PLAIN
TALK
ON

the
Epistles of John

PLAIN
TALK
ON

the
Epistles of John

MANFORD GEORGE GUTZKE
PH.D.

ZONDERVAN
PUBLISHING HOUSE

OF THE ZONDERVAN CORPORATION
GRAND RAPIDS, MICHIGAN 49506

PLAIN TALK ON THE EPISTLES OF JOHN

© 1977 by The Zondervan Corporation
Grand Rapids, Michigan

Library of Congress Cataloging in Publication Data

Gutzke, Manford George.
    Plain talk on the Epistles of John.

    1. Bible.   N.T. Epistles of John — Commentaries.
I. Title.
BS2805.3.G87   227'.94'06   77-21942
ISBN 0-310-25631-3

Printed in the United States of America

CONTENTS

PLAIN
TALK
ON

the
Epistles of John

Chapter 1

THERE IS JOY IN CHRIST JESUS

If a person accepted Jesus Christ as Savior, is there anything else he must know in order to have the fullness of blessing from God?

The First Epistle of John is a letter to believers, those who believe in Jesus Christ. When a person believes in Jesus Christ and becomes a child of God, the Bible speaks of him as a newborn babe; he is a babe in Christ. In his Epistle the apostle Peter wrote, "As newborn babes, desire the sincere milk of the word, that ye may grow thereby" (1 Peter 2:2). The Word of God is vital to Christian growth, enabling believing persons to learn more about Jesus Christ as they become more committed to Him in the Holy Spirit. In this way they will be more yielded to Him and will understand Him better. So you see, the believer grows by learning about Jesus Christ and drawing nearer to Him.

What happens as a believer grows in knowledge and in grace? In this First Epistle John emphasizes that as the believer grows in knowledge and grace, he enters more and more into fellowship with God. He is drawn to other believers and enters into the comradeship that exists among those who believe in Jesus Christ. Fellowship with the Father and with others who love Him is a source of great joy to the believer. And that is what John's Epistle is written to reveal.

That which was from the beginning, which we have heard, which we have seen with our eyes, which we have

looked upon, and our hands have handled, of the Word of
life; (for the life was manifested, and we have seen it, and
bear witness, and show unto you that eternal life, which
was with the Father, and was manifested unto us;) that
which we have seen and heard declare we unto you, that
ye also may have fellowship with us: and truly our fellowship is with the Father, and with his Son Jesus Christ.
And these things write we unto you, that your joy may be
full (1 John 1:1–4).

"That which was from the beginning, which we have heard,
. . . seen, . . . handled" is Jesus Christ, the incarnation of the
Son of God, the Word made flesh. John goes on to say, "The life
was revealed, and we have seen Him and bear witness and
proclaim to you that eternal life which was with the Father and
was revealed to us." John is drawing attention to the important
fact that the eternal life of God had become incarnate in Jesus
Christ.

Consider what is meant by eternal life. Eternal life is not our
human life continuing indefinitely forever and ever. Rather it
is the special term given to the life of God, in contrast to life of
man. My life is different in that it is temporal; I can die. God's
life is eternal; He never dies. This eternal life was incarnate in
Jesus of Nazareth, who took on human form and was seen in
this world as a man.

But there is more to the Incarnation than just that Jesus
lived. Something vitally significant happened when the Son
of God became incarnate as Jesus of Nazareth. He lived
and died in this world as Jesus of Nazareth, then was raised
from the dead and was taken up into heaven where He
is now the glorified Lord Jesus Christ in the presence of
God.

There is something about this fact which is so meaningful
and has such implications that if we understand it, we may
have fellowship with the Father and with each other,
fellowship that will grow deeper and be a source of great joy.
Because he wants our joy to be full in the Lord, John
has written this Epistle. Because he wants us to have those
blessings, he tells us what is necessary for us to have them. In

his Epistle he discusses the importance of understanding that Jesus of Nazareth was the Son of God, who came into this world to do the will of His Father; and in so doing He did something of such importance that when you and I understand it, we can have communion and fellowship with God and with each other.

Chapter 2

WALKING IN THE LIGHT

Do you think a person can be a believer in Christ and live the same way after he becomes a believer as he did before?

There is something about the life of Jesus of Nazareth that has much significance for a believer, and if he knows about it he can grow in grace and knowledge.

> This then is the message which we have heard of him, and declare unto you, that God is light, and in him is no darkness at all. If we say that we have fellowship with him, and walk in darkness, we lie, and do not the truth: but if we walk in the light, as he is in the light, we have fellowship one with another, and the blood of Jesus Christ his Son cleanseth us from all sin (1 John 1:5–7).

This is the course of explanation that John has taken. Remember that he said he would declare the things of the Lord Jesus Christ, and here in verse 5 he puts his finger on the truth at once. We may wonder what he means when he says, "God is light"; but we can get a good idea if we stop to consider what is meant when John speaks of darkness. Darkness is the natural state. In Genesis 1:2 we read, "Darkness was upon the face of the deep." Darkness is the absence of light; in the darkness we do not see anything. We learn in Genesis that when God began His creative work He said, "Let there be light." And this is what He does even now.

Becoming a believer is a matter of arriving at faith. Becoming a believer is not a matter of living in a certain fashion; it is possible only through faith in the Lord Jesus Christ. We shall see before we are through studying 1 John that this will mean a complete change in a man's life, not only because he thinks differently but also because he is depending on Someone besides himself. In any case, it can be simply stated: We start out in darkness, and we become children of God as the light shines into our hearts.

Paul talked about this:

> For God, who commanded the light to shine out of darkness, hath shined in our hearts, to give the light of the knowledge of the glory of God in the face of Jesus Christ (2 Cor. 4:6).

In Paul's own life it was God who brought light into his heart. God is the Mover; He is the One who takes the initiative. This is what God did when He said, "Let there be light: and there was light." It is well for us to keep in mind that everything God does is authentic. I may respond, and in my response I may feel as if I am acting, but I must remember that I am only responding to something already working within me; and that which is already working in me comes from God.

Remember, darkness comes first. Darkness comes naturally, then God shines into it with Himself — and there is light. Thus natural man is in darkness, as Saul the Pharisee was. When God's light comes, it is like turning on the lights in a room. So it was with Saul, and so it is with all of us. When John said, "God is light, and in him is no darkness at all," he meant that when God is present, everything lights up; when God comes into my life, it is changed completely. John says that if we have fellowship with God, we will be in the light.

When God comes, there is no darkness left. "If we say that we have fellowship with him, and walk in darkness, we lie, and do not the truth." If we claim we belong to Him while our conduct is in darkness, we are lying. How would we know what is meant by "in darkness" — what would "walking in darkness" be? It would be anything done from the human standpoint, or with the human angle in it, in human dimension. When God is in our hearts, we do not act in a human, natural way; we act as God wants us to act. We are affected by God.

The reason John can say so bluntly that we lie and "do not the truth" is something like this: If a person came to me and said, "I turned the lights on," but I could see the room was dark, I would say, "But the room is dark." He would then say, "But I turned them on. The lights are on." If one says the lights are on and another sees the room is dark, someone is lying. If we claim to be living in the Lord and walking with Christ, but our conduct is of a human sort, we lie.

John goes on to write: "But if we walk in the light, as he is in the light, we have fellowship one with another, and the blood of Jesus Christ his Son cleanseth us from all sin" (v. 7). If we live our lives as affected by the presence of God — walking in the light as Jesus Christ walked in the light, doing what God wants us to do — then it is true that we belong to Him. We will then seek communion with others who also believe and we will have fellowship because our faith in the Lord Jesus Christ makes us brothers.

This last statement, "the blood of Jesus Christ his Son cleanseth us from all sin," will be mentioned often in this Epistle. It refers to more than the historical event at Calvary. Christ's death on the cross justified us before God; it carried our guilt away and set us free.

Christ Jesus died two thousand years ago on Calvary's cross, but with God there is no such thing as time. Jesus' death is as real to God today as it was two thousand years ago. He is the eternal present. Therefore, the dying of the Lord Jesus Christ right now cleanses us from all sin. It is actually the basis for forgiving us and delivering us from sin now. Not only is there an effect right now because Jesus died on Calvary's cross, but there is also an effect on us for the future. His death on the cross makes it possible for you and me to be delivered from sin. When John says, "God is light, and in him is no darkness at all," he is saying that God makes the difference.

When we come into fellowship with God, everything is different — as different as day is from night. And "if we walk in the light, as he is in the light," and we personally live with God the way Jesus of Nazareth lived with God, "we have fellowship one with another" and the blood of Jesus Christ cleanses us from all sin. Thus, when Jesus died on Calvary, something was done for us that is still being done to this day. We shall be thinking about that in the next chapter.

Chapter 3

SIN FORGIVEN AND CLEANSED

Inasmuch as it is the most natural thing in the world for man to sin, how can any man walk with God?

As we look at verses 8 and 9 in chapter 1 of 1 John, let us keep in mind why John wrote this letter. He wrote it to believers so that they might grow in their spiritual experience and enter into more and more fellowship with God and with each other. Thus they would have greater joy. The more we concentrate on our spiritual life, the better off we are. The more attention we give to it, the better will be the results and the more happiness and joy we will have.

John wrote to declare the truth that was set forth in Jesus Christ. We shall find that John dwells on the fact that God came in human form, lived here in this world in human form, died and was raised from the dead in that human form, and ascended into heaven in that human form, thereby opening the way for us to come into fellowship with God.

John speaks of all the truth of God as light. This means that the human being by himself is in darkness; anyone who lives in just the human way is in darkness.

What does that mean? The natural man does not have the life of God in him. Some people think that God works in them through nature. That is true in one sense, but what God does in the natural processes is not the truth that is in Jesus Christ. What God does in the natural processes is what is covered by law, but what God will do for us in Christ Jesus is an extension of His grace toward us. This is what John points out. He says that God is light, and in Him there is no darkness at all; the life of God is a complete life and there is no human element. John is writing to declare the truth in Jesus Christ so that believers, understanding it better, may live more intelligently, joyfully becoming closer to God, to Jesus Christ, and to each other.

John goes on at this point to say:

> If we say that we have no sin, we deceive ourselves, and the truth is not in us. If we confess our sins, he is faithful and just to forgive us our sins, and to cleanse us from all unrighteousness (1 John 1:8,9).

If anyone claims that he has no sin, that he does not need cleansing, he is deceiving himself. What difference does this make? If someone thinks he is all right, he'll become complacent and not do anything about his condition; but if he realizes that he is a sinner and knows that as a sinner he will never make it, then he will turn to salvation and receive the Savior. For that reason, of course, the Bible will undertake to show that sin is so common that the entire world is guilty before God and must turn to the Lord Jesus Christ for salvation.

There is no question about the reality of our sins; the question is, What are we going to do about them? There are just two things we can do. We can either try to cover them up and not mention them, or we can openly confess them. Proverbs 28:13 tells us that "he that covereth his sins shall not prosper." But he who "confesseth and forsaketh them shall have mercy." God will always be faithful, and He will keep the covenant promise He made to His Son, Jesus Christ.

The Bible indicates that when God's Son came into this world, He came with an understanding that if He would die for sinners, those who put their trust in Him would be saved. This plan was revealed several times in the prayers of Jesus of Nazareth.

Here John says, "If we confess our sins, he is faithful and just." *Just* means "fair"; it means He will do the right thing. In what sense can He be fair when He forgives my sins? Jesus died for my sins, so my sins have been paid for. Then I should not die for them. In other words, if Christ paid the bill, God would not collect from me twice. That would not be fair. And He is fair. Christ Jesus died for me, so I go free.

When we say the Lord God forgives us our sins, we do not want anyone to get the idea that God would say, "Oh, that's all right. We will just overlook the fact that you made a mistake." Since God has His laws, He could not do that and be fair. The truth is, "the soul that sinneth, it shall die." Then how is He going to be able to save us? The gospel deals with this: He will forgive us, and the word *forgive* means that sin will be canceled out and not remembered any more against us. "He is faithful and just to forgive us our sins."

Because Christ Jesus died for us and because we believe in Him, the blood of Jesus Christ cleanses us from all sins and takes them away. Even so, He is faithful and just to forgive us our sins and to cleanse us from all unrighteousness. "Cleansing us from all unrighteousness" is an operational term meaning He sets us free. This marvelous truth is not just wishful thinking; this is what is actually done in and through and by Jesus Christ. So remarkable is the work of Jesus Christ, and so wonderful is His power, that if we yield ourselves into His hands, God will through Him deliver us completely. He is able to set us free from the sin that has held us back in the past.

We must keep in mind that John is writing to believers to tell them that their whole spiritual life is tied up with Jesus Christ. He wants them to understand what Christ has done for them. He also wants them to understand that God is able freely and fully, faithfully and fairly, to forgive their sins and to cleanse them from all unrighteousness. What Jesus Christ did when He died for us was such that, as far as God is concerned, He became committed to setting us free. We actually are among those who are freed from their sins.

Chapter 4

SIN DENIED

If a man says that he can come to God just as he is, do you realize that he is making it unnecessary for Jesus Christ to have come, and that this is making a liar out of Him?

In this study of the First Epistle of John we will now be considering verse 10 in the first chapter. This verse brings to our minds the importance of the apostles' teaching. You may be asking yourself the question we have been considering: If you are already a believer in the Lord Jesus Christ, why should you study the Bible? The answer is simple. The more you understand the Bible, the more you will believe the gospel, and the more you believe the gospel, the more blessing you will have — and this brings joy. That is the end toward which the Lord Jesus Christ came — that you and I might be saved into the fullness of joy in Him.

A good understanding of Christ and His work comes from the study of His Word. Consider the meaning of the Word: "If we say that we have not sinned, we make him a liar, and his word is not in us." That is a simple, straightforward statement. If we take the position that our lives are as they ought to be, and that we have not done anything that would be considered wrong, we make Christ a liar.

John is pointing out in this Epistle the basis on which we can come to God. Every apostle, minister, missionary, and personal worker who talks about the things of Christ is seeking to show people how to come to God. When parents teach their children about the gospel, they show them how they can come to God. Many times we feel that we go to church and Sunday school to be told how to come to God and what to do in His sight.

In Sunday school the Ten Commandments are taught and children learn that this is the will of God for them. But that is not all: they find out not only what God requires of them, but also what God will do for them when they have done wrong. The salvation work of God is revealed in the gospel, and this is what John is declaring. He wants to show how a sinner can come to God. Basically John's approach in this Epistle is that we can come to God because the Son of God became incarnate as Jesus of Nazareth and opened the way for us. The truth in Jesus Christ is necessary for the salvation of our souls. John is declaring that the whole ground on which we can come to God is based on the fact that Jesus Christ was the incarnate Son of God. If we ask ourselves why He became incarnate, we will find in Scripture that He took on the nature of man so that He might die.

> But we see Jesus, who was made a little lower than the angels for the suffering of death, crowned with glory and honour; that he by the grace of God should taste death for every man. For it became him, for whom are all things, and by whom are all things, in bringing many sons unto glory, to make the captain of their salvation perfect through sufferings (Heb. 2:9,10).

The writer of this Epistle dwells on this truth with even greater emphasis when he writes:

> Forasmuch then as the children are partakers of flesh and blood, he also himself likewise took part of the same; that through death he might destroy him that had the power of death, that is, the devil; and deliver them who through fear of death were all their lifetime subject to bondage. For verily he took not on him the nature of angels; but he took on him the seed of Abraham (2:14–16).

When God sent His Son into the world to save us, He did not send Him as an angel, because an angel could not have died. God sent Him as a man because His death was necessary to provide our redemption.

It is recorded in the Gospels that Jesus of Nazareth said the Son of Man came "not to be ministered unto, but to minister, and to give his life a ransom for many." Jesus, when talking to the disciples on the road to Emmaus after His resurrection, said to them, "Ought not Christ to have suffered these things, and to enter into his glory?" (Luke 24:26). The Scripture makes it plain that He became incarnate; He was born as a human being in order that He might die. Now we can answer the question, Why did He need to die? Because of our sin. That is all there is to it. "The soul that sinneth, it shall die," and so we were condemned to death; but Christ Jesus came and died for us. He took our place so that in Him we might be free.

His coming in the form of flesh to die was necessary because sin is real. If sin had not been real, His death would not have been necessary. But sin was a barrier between God and ourselves. John wants his readers to understand this clearly: "If we say that we have not sinned [if we take the position we have not done anything wrong; if we claim that in the sight of God our consciences are clear and that we are all right in the sight of God], we make Him [Jesus Christ] a liar." In what sense? In the very fact that He came to save us, which is ridiculous unless we were lost. He came to die for us, which was not necessary unless we were doomed to death. He came to save us from our sins, which was not necessary unless we have sinned.

If we say that we can have fellowship with God just because God is kind, so that we can come to Him without needing the sacrificial death of His Son, we are making Christ Jesus a liar. He came to die for us, which would be foolish unless we needed this kind of sacrifice on our behalf. If I claim I have not sinned, I am not thinking the thoughts of Jesus Christ. If my outlook on life is that I am doing all right in my own efforts, then I make Christ Jesus a fool, because He came for me. It would be as if someone came to help me when I did not need help. How foolish would a man look if he came running into the house with a fire extinguisher when there was no fire. That is how foolish it would be if Christ Jesus had died for people who did not need it.

Christ Jesus came into this world to seek and to save the lost. He came to give His life as a ransom for many. He came not to be ministered unto, but to minister. He came that He might suffer for us, even as He taught, "Ought not Christ to have suffered and to have been raised from the dead?" However, all of this is useless and meaningless unless we have faith. John is stressing here that we should be honest and candid about our daily life and about our personal selves. We should admit in the presence of God that we are not good enough for His presence. Elsewhere in the Bible this would be called "repentance." We would say that a man has to repent and believe the gospel, "repentance" being that he acknowledges that he has done wrong, and "believing in the gospel" is when he accepts Jesus Christ as his Savior.

Chapter 5

CHRIST OUR ADVOCATE

When a man sins, must he face Almighty God alone?

> My little children, these things write I unto you, that ye
> sin not (1 John 2:1).

What John really means is that everything he is doing, all he is
writing in the entire Epistle is actually to help believers not to
sin.

> And if any man sin, we have an advocate with the Father,
> Jesus Christ the righteous: and he is the propitiation for
> our sins: and not for ours only, but also for the sins of the
> whole world (1 John 2:1,2).

So John is writing this epistle of explanation to help believers
not to sin — the better they understand the grace of God, the
less they will sin. To begin with, the more a believer understands what Christ has done for him, the less he will want to
sin. The more he understands the grace of God that is available, the less he will need to sin. He can actually be delivered
from sin.

In his whole discussion John is satisfied that if he writes
about these things and believers heed what he has written, the
result will be that they will be less inclined to disobey God, and
they will be more inclined to walk in the ways of God. Then
John goes on to say, "If any man sin [in spite of everything that
has been done in the gospel], we have an advocate with the
Father, Jesus Christ the righteous." Now this word *advocate* is
well known. An advocate is a lawyer who appears in court on

behalf of his client; he is a defense lawyer. An accused person calls on him to advocate his defense. When John says believers have an advocate with the Father, he means they have a defense lawyer in court: Jesus Christ, who is perfect in the sight of God, who enjoys good relations with God the Father, God the Father said about Jesus: "Thou art my beloved Son; in thee I am well pleased."

Jesus Christ, then, is the believer's Advocate, the believer's Representative. So whenever a believer does anything wrong, he has Someone in the presence of God representing him; and the Person representing him never did anything wrong. Jesus Christ is the perfect man; and He is the propitiation for sins, the One who reconciles men to God. He makes it possible for God to deal with believers as though they had not sinned.

Many people wonder whether or not the death of Jesus Christ was for everyone or only for those who believe in Him. I think we can say in one sense He died for all men, and in another sense He died for the people who believe in Him. Perhaps the best way to say it is that He died for whosoever will come to Him. The invitation is as wide as the human race. Anyone anywhere, whosoever will, let him come and take of the water of life freely.

Not everyone will come. Believing in the Lord Jesus Christ is not only a matter of hearing the gospel; it is receiving it for oneself and committing oneself to it. We can therefore say that Jesus came to die for those who believe in Him. But John here goes on to say "not for ours only." In other words, Christ offered Himself to take the burden of the responsibility and to carry the guilt away not only for those who believe, but also for the whole world. That is something we must emphasize in our preaching. In order to receive the blessing of the Lord Jesus Christ, whosoever will, let him come; whosoever comes He will not cast out.

John is writing about the believer — one who believes the Lord Jesus Christ is the Son of God, and who understands that Christ died for him and has received Him as his Savior. To the best of his knowledge he has committed the keeping of himself to Jesus Christ, and he expects to be brought into the presence of God, forgiven and cleansed and made fit, by the grace of God in Christ Jesus. There are some who do not believe in the Lord Jesus Christ as a Helper. My heart goes out to those who believe in the life of the Lord Jesus Christ as desirable, who might even believe in His teaching as true and in His conduct as desirable, but who then try to live in their own strength. John would say to these people that when this happens, they will not be able to do it.

I do not know how many people think that being a Christian means doing the right thing, and that if you want to be a Christian you make up your mind to go to church, where they tell you what to do, and then you do it. But what being a Christian really means is receiving Jesus Christ by taking Him as your personal Savior, hearing the truth of the Lord Jesus Christ, believing it to be true, and committing the keeping of your soul to Him. This is what John wants to happen to everyone.

Are you among those who believe in the Lord Jesus Christ? If this is not settled in your mind, why don't you decide right now that you are going to get this straightened out? You may actually be one of those for whom Christ died and who could receive the benefit. Somewhere among your acquaintances there is a real believer. Go to him and let him help you receive Jesus Christ.

Chapter 6

BELONGING TO CHRIST

How can a person know that he truly is a Christian?

In the experience of believing in Christ Jesus, our personal relationship with Him is a matter of faith, so that our belonging to Him is something we understand in our consciousness. There is no outward sign. I sometimes think that if the matter of becoming a believer was as easy as getting into a car, or perhaps going into a church and knowing that you are inside, we could understand it more easily. This matter of receiving the Lord Jesus Christ, however, is something that takes place in our hearts, in our consciousness; and because it does, and because we are the kind of people we are, there are times when we wonder if it really did happen. It is like finally making up your mind about something; if outwardly nothing is changed and it is just a matter of being in your mind, then two or three days afterwards you may wonder, "Did I or didn't I? Is it real or isn't it?" And this experience undoubtedly comes to professing believers.

As long as you and I have any doubts in our minds that we really do belong to the Lord, it hurts our spiritual experience because it weakens our confidence. We do not follow Him closely if we are not sure that we belong to Him. Unless in our own hearts we are fully persuaded that we belong to the Lord, and unless we have confidence about our relationship with Him, our personal spiritual experience and our faith will be weak.

Some Christians have an emotional experience, after which

they feel they know for sure about their relationship with Christ. But it is possible that for some of us there is no special emotional experience. We know in our hearts and minds that we understand about the Lord and we receive Him. Later we may wonder: Do we or don't we really belong? Did we or didn't we really accept the Lord? This particular problem is faced by John as he writes:

> And hereby we do know that we know him, if we keep his commandments (1 John 2:3).

The second use of the word *know* means that we accept Christ as our Savior and yield to Him as our Lord. We trust in Him, esteem Him, and honor Him. John goes on to say:

> He that saith, I know him, and keepeth not his com- mandments, is a liar, and the truth is not in him. But whoso keepeth his word, in him verily is the love of God perfected: hereby know we that we are in him (1 John 2:4,5).

Let us look at this more closely. The statement "Hereby we do know that we know him, if we keep his commandments" is not so much a matter of obeying specific rules. This reference to "keeping his commandments" is a general term. If we intend to obey and follow Him, God will offer us guidance. The word *keep* means to cherish, to prevent from being broken, as if keeping His commandments were like handling a delicate piece of china: it would be given special care and not subjected to rough treatment. Here is the evidence, the practical sign, that we do believe in Him: when there is within us the inward disposition to obey Him.

> He that saith, I know him, and keepeth not his com- mandments, is a liar, and the truth is not in him (1 John 2:4).

That is a definite statement, and we wonder how John can be so positive, and why he would say it so bluntly. The reason is simple. The person who says that he knows the Lord — that he is honoring and accepting Christ as Lord and Savior — but is not seeking to obey the will of God is, according to John, a liar. He is making a false claim and the truth is not operative in him.

John states that such action is marked by inconsistency. If a person says that he knows Christ and does not keep His commandments, he is like a person saying that he is in the sunlight but cannot see anything, or that he is standing in a pool of water but claims he is not wet. That does not make sense. If we truly recognize Jesus as Lord and allow His Holy Spirit to live in us, we will have within us the disposition to do His will. "Whoso keepeth his word, in him verily is the love of God perfected." Such a person really wants to obey God, and he cherishes guidance from God. He obeys the Word and does what God wants him to do.

Perfected means "brought to its fullness," "brought to harvest." When a person sincerely wants to obey the Lord, the love of God is brought to its proper end. Whoever is obedient to God, who wants to do what is pleasing in His sight, has the proof within him, and in him the love of God is perfected. And here we have before us the answer to the question that we raised at the outset. If a Christian wonders whether or not he belongs to the Lord, wonders whether or not his faith is real, he can ask himself one question: Is he inwardly anxious to be sure that he is well-pleasing in the sight of God, or does he just think, "I'll do what I can, and I hope that nothing happens that will make me look bad." Whenever I do something just because others are doing it or say it is the right thing to do, while I personally consider it to be evil, that is evidence that the truth of God is not operative in me.

In other words, Christ Jesus died for us and was raised from the dead for us, that we may have eternal life in Him. All of that is truth; and if we know that, it will affect us in such a way that we will inwardly want to obey the Word of God. The very fact that we now belong to the Lord and that He is in us will be revealed in the fact that just as the Lord Jesus did everything to please the Father when He was in this world, so will we want to do the things that will please the Father.

Chapter 7

EVIDENCE OF A REGENERATED HEART

If a person is a believer in Christ, can you tell by his behavior? Is there a certain something he would be doing if he were a believer?

In 1 John 2 we will see that there is a way in which a person can tell whether he truly is a Christian:

> He that saith he abideth in him ought himself also so to walk, even as he walked (1 John 2:6).

This does not mean that such a man should make up his mind to walk in the ways of the Lord, rather it means that such a man will *already* be walking in the ways of the Lord. Say, for example, that I am in the backyard, and you see me across the fence. You ask what I am doing. It happens that there is a man by the name of Mr. Brown working in the garden; so I say that I am working with Mr. Brown. If I say I am working with Mr. Brown, what can you expect me to be doing? You can expect that I am working in the garden, because Mr. Brown is working in the garden. If I say that I am working with Mr. Brown, but you find me sitting in the shade reading a book, then something is wrong with what I said.

This is John's point here. When we say that we are abiding in the Lord Jesus Christ, we do not mean that we have any personal relation to His physical body. When we are abiding in Him, we are following Him. In other words, we are obeying and trusting in Him. And anyone who claims that ought to be walking just as the Lord Jesus walked. This should follow naturally.

> Brethren, I write no new commandment unto you, but an old commandment which ye had from the beginning (1 John 2:7).

This matter of doing the will of God, as the Lord Jesus is doing the will of God, is not new. This was always the plan of God. Man was created to obey God, to walk with Him. If you look back to the creation of man, you will find that man was not created to act by himself. God created man for Himself, and man was to come to Him. God made it man's responsibility to obey Him. God put man into this world and told him what to do. That was from the beginning.

That is exactly what the Lord Jesus did. When He came into this world, He did the will of His Father. Human beings in their sin do not do the will of God; however, the believer does, because he lets the will of the Lord Jesus Christ prevail in his heart. If I am walking as Jesus walked, which will include self-denial and obedience to God, that is the way God intended from the first that I should walk. The Lord Jesus said when He was here in this world: "I do nothing of myself. My Father worketh hitherto, and I work" (John 8:28; 5:17). That would have been God's original plan for man, and Jesus Christ actually carried it out.

John goes on to say:

> The old commandment is the word which ye have heard from the beginning (1 John 2:7).

That was the original plan. God made man and the garden; then He put the man into the garden and told him to dress it and keep it. Man had the responsibility to do these things.

> Again, a new commandment I write unto you, which thing is true in him and in you: because the darkness is past, and the true light now shineth (1 John 2:8).

This appears to be a contradiction but it isn't. John is saying that there is an aspect in which the commandment is new, and the new aspect is that the truth itself is carried out in Him and in you. The will of God was performed first in Jesus of Nazareth, and now in the believer. It was the will of God from the first that man should obey Him. Man did not do it. But when Jesus was born in human form, He did obey. Those of us who are in the Lord Jesus Christ also obey God and keep His commandments. This is the new aspect of the truth.

> Because the darkness is past, and the true light now shineth (1 John 2:8).

Here John uses the word *darkness* to refer to the sinfulness of man, or man's self-will: the tendency on man's part to do as he sees fit. But, John says, "the darkness is past." No longer need man grope in sin, darkness, self-will. The will of God has been manifested in Jesus Christ. The darkness is past and the true light now shines. True obedience to God can be seen in Jesus Christ and is now available to us.

John goes on to illustrate:

> He that saith he is in the light, and hateth his brother, is in darkness even until now (1 John 2:9).

This is the same as the person claiming to be walking in the light when he is in darkness: he is not telling the truth. Anyone who claims to be obeying God when he is not seeking the welfare of other human beings is actually still living in the sinful disobedience of his own self-will. To claim that the life of God is working in me while I am not seeking the welfare of other human beings is actually proof that I am really living in my own willfulness and disobedience to God. If I know what I am saying, I am just plain lying, because he who says he is in the light — the person who claims to be living in obedience to God — and hates his brother is in darkness even until now. He is still in disobedience, because it is characteristic of God that He does not hate the people He created. He seeks their welfare.

> He that loveth his brother abideth in the light, and there is none occasion of stumbling in him (1 John 2:10).

"Abiding in the light" means living in the light. "The light" is obedience to God, doing His will. A person who loves his brother is actually abiding in the light because he is doing God's will. He will never hinder anyone from coming to the Lord, and everyone who sees him will give God the glory.

But he that hateth his brother is in darkness, and walketh
in darkness, and knoweth not whither he goeth, because
that darkness hath blinded his eyes (1 John 2:11).

Anyone who is not seeking the welfare of other human beings,
and whose outward life shows that he is selfish, is still living in
his own sinful disobedience, which John would call darkness.
He is still living and walking in darkness, and he doesn't know
where he is going, because that is a feature of being in the dark.

We are reminded of the occasion when the Lord Jesus
prayed on the cross: "Father, forgive them; for they know not
what they do." The darkness had blinded their eyes. Often a
person who is not a believer, who does not want to obey God
and has no interest in doing His will, cannot even see what is
wrong. Darkness has blinded his eyes. To be without concern
for the welfare of others is to live in sinful disobedience. We
used to say, "There is none so blind as those that will not see."
If a person will not see what God wants him to do, he is blind.
And John would say that if you are a believer, you will walk in
the ways of God and be interested in the welfare of other
people.

Chapter 8

A GODLY WALK

If a person wanted to live in the will of God, could he do it in his own strength? Can just anyone live as Jesus of Nazareth lived?

In our study of 1 John, we have been considering the matter of knowing whether or not a person is a believer. John has raised the question, How can you tell that you actually are a believer in the Lord Jesus Christ? We will now see that this matter of living as a believer is possible only if you have had the experience of being saved. While it is true that a believer is a human being who walks with the Lord and obeys Him, this is not a simple matter. Not everyone is free to walk with the Lord. Not everyone could obey Him even if he wanted to do so. Sometimes people get the impression that being a believer is just a matter of choice, then if a person wanted to live as a believer, he could do it. In a sense this is true. Any person can be a believer if he wants to be one, but it will be under certain conditions and in certain ways. That person will need to have the experience that we call salvation.

> I write unto you, little children, because your sins are forgiven you for his name's sake (1 John 2:12).

"Little children" refers to souls who have just become believers, like "babes in Christ"; and it is also an endearing word — the kind of word that would be spoken in a loving way by an older person. John has been urging believers to walk as Christ walked. They should walk in the light as He is in the light. They should be interested in the welfare of others.

John says he is writing this way because their sins have been forgiven for Christ's name's sake. Actually if a person did not have his sins forgiven, he would not want to walk this way, because in his own heart and mind he would still be on the defensive, trying to justify himself. But if a person's sins are forgiven and he knows there is nothing held against him, he has nothing to defend, and he is willing to do the will of God even in the matter of caring for other people. John emphasizes that the forgiveness of sins was "for the sake of the Lord Jesus Christ." This means that Christ Jesus has died for sinners, and God is able now to forgive believers their sins because His Son paid the penalty.

> I write unto you, fathers, because ye have known him that is from the beginning (1 John 2:13a).

The word *fathers* refers to mature Christians. John is saying, "I am writing unto you mature believers because you have seen and have appreciated what God had in mind from the very beginning when He created the heaven and the earth." He says, "I have written unto you mature believers because you have known Him that is from the beginning. You have honored and respected God from the very first."

> I write unto you, young men, because ye have overcome the wicked one (1 John 2:13b).

We observe that John is writing to some believers who are young in their faith. As new converts, they are strong and vigorous and in their prime, and they have overcome the wicked one. This means they are free. Before this they were in bondage to Satan, but the Lord Jesus came into this world to destroy the works of the devil. He died to open the way for the believer to be delivered from sin. The way being opened, the believer actually overcomes the wicked one in his life.

> I write unto you, little children, because ye have known the Father (1 John 2:13c).

John tells the new believers, "You have known the Father. You have respected and appreciated that relationship with God as Father and you as His child. You have learned that in Christ you were included in the family of God. You could not have known God as Father if you had not known Jesus Christ the Son, because the Bible reports that Jesus said, 'All things are delivered to me of my Father: and no man knoweth who the Son is, but the Father; and who the Father is, but the Son, and he to whom the Son will reveal him' (Luke 10:22)."

> I have written unto you, fathers, because ye have known him that is from the beginning (1 John 2:14a).

This is a repetition of verse 13; John tells mature believers, "You have understood and appreciated that which was from the very beginning of creation; you have this picture in mind and it makes you strong."

> I have written unto you, young men, because ye are strong, and the word of God abideth in you, and ye have overcome the wicked one (1 John 2:14b).

This is an even stronger passage than verse 13. It brings out the idea that these young men have overcome the wicked one and have been delivered from the power of Satan.

You will remember that Paul was commissioned to open the eyes of the blind and deliver them from the power of Satan into the power of God. These young men had been so delivered. Having been delivered from the power of Satan, they could be strong in their freedom. The revealed will of God is operative in them as they continue to achieve victories over the enemy. As long as the believer practices the crucifixion of the flesh (if he will reckon his flesh indeed to be dead), he is continually overcoming Satan. And this will happen if the Word of God abides in him. "The word of God abideth in you, and ye have overcome the wicked one." Being delivered by death and the resurrection in his own personal experience, he is strong and will receive eagerly the will of God in his life. He can have continual victory over the malicious darts of the enemy by putting his trust in Jesus Christ. This is what John has been saying: Only the saved walk in the light. The believer will know he is a believer if he desires to do the will of God. How would a believer act in doing the will of God? He would have his heart and interest in the welfare of people other than himself; he would love others.

Can just anyone love the Lord? No, and there are a number of reasons why. If a person is still in his guilt and realizes that God will deal with him as with a guilty sinner, he will not be inclined to be gracious to other people. If he is going to be called into account, he will call others into account. If a person feels that God will deal with him on the basis of his sin, his attitude toward other people is to make them pay for everything they have done wrong. He would be inclined to say they can look out for themselves. None of that is of the Lord. But if the person believes that God has forgiven him so that his sins are forgiven, he will be ready to deal with other people graciously, because that is the way God has dealt with him. So the answer to the question Can anyone live the Christian life? is that a person must first be saved to live the life of a believer. He must be forgiven, and for that he must know about the Lord Jesus Christ Himself. He must know how to overcome the wicked one. He must have fellowship with the Lord and walk with Him.

Chapter 9

LOOK TO GOD

When I am trying to make up my mind as to what I should do, should I think of doing what I want to do, or should I think of doing what God would want me to do?

In the second chapter of this Epistle, John considers the matter of our knowing for sure that we belong to God. It would seem from the way John is writing this portion of the Epistle that he realizes how important it is for us to know for sure. We need to know that we have been forgiven and that we are members of the body of Christ, and of the family of God, so we might have the confidence which will strengthen us in our living and give us joy.

Much in life is decided by the way we feel. We are often faced with the fact that we could do differently; the choice to decide which way to go is a daily affair. Many of these choices are directly related to ourselves. In other words, I always have *myself* to deal with, and when I think about what is to be done, I invariably think about what it will mean to me. In any given situation that I am conscious of, the real issue is "I." In general I could say that the issue in question will develop in my life according to whether I seek what I can get or what I can give in any given situation.

John approaches this entire issue in a rather negative way. He says, "Love not the world, neither the things that are in the world." Everything around me might be known as "the world," and in this situation there are many appealing things that I would like for myself. So the situation I am in presents a challenge: a challenge to get out of it what I can. John would call that "loving the world." On the other hand, I could in the same situation check in my mind to see what I could do to serve God. I will have to think in terms of whether I am going to serve myself or God; and when I love the world and the things in the world, I am actually serving myself.

> Love not the world, neither the things that are in the world. If any man love the world, the love of the Father is not in him (1 John 2:15).

This is John's way of saying that we should not allow ourselves to have or to enjoy or to advance the interests of that which is in the world. If anyone gives himself over to serve what the world presents before him, it is obvious he is not giving himself to serve God. This is a way of saying there is only one of me, and if I give myself over to serve "me," then that is the end of "me." I could give myself over to serve God, but I cannot do both. No man can serve two masters.

> For all that is in the world, the lust of the flesh, and the lust of the eyes, and the pride of life, is not of the Father, but is of the world (1 John 2:16).

In those three things that have been listed there are three avenues along which I am personally interested — things that appeal to me. The word *lust* here means strong desires, not necessarily evil, although they could quickly and easily lead into evil. The lust of the flesh is the strong desire of my human nature, the general feeling I have when I look at anything and think "that would feel good to me." Thus it becomes something desirable, and when all is added up, we have what we call my appetite. The appetite might be food, pleasure, interest of any sort, whether it be in making money or having fun, and so on: that which is pleasing to me.

The second one, "the lust of the eyes," is the strong desire of my imagination, when I want something because it looks good to me. Sometimes things do not feel good, but they look good; and their appeal to me thus becomes a matter of imagination.

And third is the pride of life: vanity, the interest in self that whenever I look at something, I think "that would really set me up." These three ideas — appetite, imagination, and vanity — all refer to *me*. Such interests do not originate from God — they originate in my own sinful heart, from my ego. They are basically selfish. They are not in the will of Christ; they are my will for myself.

Jesus of Nazareth could say, "I do nothing of myself." When He said that, He ended the whole business. The lust of the flesh did not appeal to Him: when He was tempted to turn the stones into bread, He refused to do so. The lust of the eyes did not appeal to Him: when taken up and shown all the kingdoms of the world in a moment of time, He refused to accept Satan's offer. You remember He was asked to take Himself to the top of a tall cliff and throw Himself down to show people that He really was the Son of God. This kind of action would have made Him vain. But He refused all the temptations in the wilderness.

> And the world passeth away, and the lust thereof: but he
> that doeth the will of God abideth for ever (1 John 2:17).

Just as flowers wilt and wither, things that appeal to our vanity do not last long; but John says that whoever does the will of God abides forever. All of the selfish things that appeal to us are in themselves temporary, whether they be food, pleasures, or sensations of any kind — anything that is a matter of delight as far as our physical bodies are concerned. It is a case of "he that drinketh of this water shall thirst again." They will all fade away, but whatever is done in obedience to God is eternal. Eternal things are gained by responding to the eternal life that is within us by the will of Christ.

If we believe in the Lord Jesus Christ, receive Him as our Lord and Savior, yield to Him as the One who will control us from within, and let His Holy Spirit show us the things of God, He will move us to do the will of the Father. If you and I seek to do the will of the Father, that will never end. The things we do for Him are eternally important. In that way we can actually live our lives in such a way that, while dealing with temporal things in this world, we are really laying up for ourselves treasure in heaven. John would say to us about our living that as we are making decisions and choices, we should not do what appeals to us personally, but what appeals to God.

Chapter 10

CHRIST: THE ONLY WAY

If we say there is only one gospel of the Lord Jesus Christ, how should we feel about those who claim that we can come to God some other way?

In this study of 1 John we have been thinking about how we can be sure we belong to the Lord. We have found that there are various problems which John considers as we go along, and now in the latter part of the second chapter we learn that this matter of being a believer is complicated because of other people. Being a believer in Christ is a matter of yielding one's self to God; we repent, deny ourselves, and trust Him. This involves death to our personal human natures that we might be raised from the dead and live in the newness of life in Christ Jesus. That is actually what is going to happen. But we have a problem with that because denying ourselves is something we are not anxious to do.

All this trouble we have in denying and committing ourselves to God in Christ Jesus is complicated by the fact that there are other people who also claim to be doing the will of God; but they do not do it this way. We are not alone in the world, and this is both good and bad. If others are going the same way we are going, it is easier to walk in the direction we want to go; but if other people are walking in different directions, it is harder to walk in the way we want to go. And that is how it is with believing in God. There are people who do not follow the gospel as it is set forth in the Bible. There are forces in the world which undertake to guide us in spiritual matters but do not attempt this in the way of the Christian gospel, in which we have the truth as it is in Christ. The truth of Christ as seen in Jesus of Nazareth sets forth the idea that the human being on earth, as Jesus was in human form, should be totally and altogether obedient to the Father who is in heaven. The Lord Jesus said, "I do nothing of myself. I do only what the Father in heaven wants me to do"; and we know the story of His life. The Father in heaven eventually wanted Him to give Himself on the cross, and this involved His death so that God might raise Him from the dead, that He might live forever. That is the truth in Christ. This requires total obedience to God even unto the death of self, in which we count on the resurrection from the dead and living in the newness of life that comes from God in the resurrection experience.

There are those who teach differently. They say that we can do the will of God without having to die; that we can do His will by living better lives. These forces which claim to do the will of God, but which do not follow the pattern of Jesus of Nazareth, are called by John "antichrists." We know that the word *Christ* is used for the truth as it is in Jesus of Nazareth, but *antichrist* is used for ideas contrary to that. Often they are far more plausible, but they are not the same as the things of the Lord Jesus Christ. This is what John is referring to when he writes:

> Little children, it is the last time: and as ye have heard that antichrist shall come, even now are there many antichrists; whereby we know that it is the last time (1 John 2:18).

What does John mean by the "last time"? I suggest that he means something like what we mean when we say "it is a showdown," the time for making a final decision. In effect, John is saying "We have heard that the antichrist is coming; there are many antichrists here right now; and since there are antichrists in the world, we know that this is the showdown. We have to make up our minds. If we are going north, we cannot go east, west, or south — only north." John has this to say about those to whom he was referring as antichrists: "They went out from us." They were not of the true believers. There are some people in the church today who claim to be believers; they use the same language, but they do not teach what we teach. We teach that the way to walk with the Lord and to obey Him is to deny ourselves entirely, to yield ourselves totally into the will of the living God, and to let God work in us to will and to do of His good pleasure.

Some of these people will claim that they are going to obey God. They do not talk much about yielding themselves to Him, and they do not talk about denying themselves. They may talk about bringing themselves in line, but they do not talk about reckoning themselves dead, and they do not talk about being crucified with Christ. However, they claim to be real believers. But John says, "They went out from us, but they were not of us." Then John argues:

> If they had been of us, they would no doubt have continued with us: but they went out, that they might be made manifest that they were not all of us (1 John 2:19).

This brings to mind something of utmost importance: Whenever there is any strong movement in the church, there will be people who are opposed to it. There are people who do not teach and preach what the Bible teaches, and they may be inside the congregation. John would say that God allows these people to be there so that believers must decide which they will follow.

If a believer should say, "I would not know what to do," John gives guidance: "But ye have an unction from the Holy One, and ye know all things" (v. 20). And here is something that the Bible brings to our attention: if you are a true believer in the Lord Jesus Christ, you will be given a way of knowing from within what is right. No one will have to tell you, and no one can take it away from you. You have an unction from the Holy One and you can inwardly know. If it is not the will of the Lord Jesus Christ, if it is not the way He did it, then it is not for you.

> I have not written unto you because ye know not the truth, but because ye know it, and that no lie is of the truth (1 John 2:21).

You know the truth and anything that contradicts the gospel of the Lord Jesus Christ is not true. "Who is a liar but he that denieth that Jesus is the Christ?" (v. 22). This refers to anyone who would deny that the truth of the story of the Lord Jesus Christ is actually the eternal way of God. The story of Jesus Christ includes the following: He was born of God; He was the Son of God incarnate in human form; God Himself was His Father; and He was born into this world that He might suffer and die and be raised from the dead and be taken into the presence of God, where He is now. In Jesus of Nazareth is God's way of doing things.

> He is antichrist, that denieth the Father and the Son
> (1 John 2:22).

Notice that when the Scripture says that he "denieth the Father and the Son," he is not denying the existence of God and Christ as such, but he is denying that God is the Father of the Lord Jesus Christ, and he is denying that Jesus of Nazareth is the Son of God. The person who has no interest in this relationship which makes God my Father and me His child is a person who does not accept the way of Christ and is actually the antichrist.

"Whosoever denieth the Son, the same hath not the Father" (v. 23). The person who does not recognize any relationship with God in Jesus Christ is antichrist. If I am regenerated, I belong to Him. Anyone who does not hold to this is denying not only the Son, but he does not have the Father, either.

> These things have I written unto you concerning them that seduce you. But the anointing which ye have received of him abideth in you, and ye need not that any man teach you: but as the same anointing teacheth you of all things, and is truth, and is no lie, and even as it hath taught you, ye shall abide in him (1 John 2:26,27).

That is the way it has been put before us. Therefore, let that which you have heard from the beginning abide in you.

Chapter 11

COMMITMENT TO CHRIST ALONE

How can a believer tell whether or not a certain teacher or preacher is a reliable person to follow?

As you listen to men present their views, do you ever have a feeling of confusion that makes you wonder which is the way to go? John wrote his First Epistle to believers to help them with this very matter. He reminded them that every sincere, believing person has been given an inward consciousness of God that will guide him as he moves forward.

> And this is the promise that he hath promised us, even eternal life (1 John 2:25).

Eternal life does not mean our human life going on forever, an unending continuation of this life. This term *eternal* life refers to the life of God, which is a new life that is in us in addition to the old life we had as human beings.

For instance, when I was born, I had the life in me that was in my father and mother: the life that all other human beings have, in scriptural terms the "life of Adam." That life is sinful. Humanly speaking, I am naturally a sinful person; but when I believe in the Lord Jesus Christ and receive Him as my Savior, God gives to me a new life. That is what we mean when we speak of the second birth. It is not the old birth over again the second time; it is a new, different birth: a new life. It is eternal life. This is what God has promised us.

John continues: "These things have I written unto you concerning them that seduce you." There he is referring to verses 18 and 19 when he talked about antichrists. He is saying they are the kind of people who confuse others. John now has something further to say about this. He has been writing to help believers to be ready to deal with people with other ideas. For them he has a word of assurance.

> But the anointing which ye have received of him abideth
> in you (1 John 2:27).

When John uses the word *anointing,* there will immediately come to mind the experience of receiving the Holy Spirit. We should not be afraid of the biblical term "the baptism of the Holy Spirit," for the Lord Jesus was to baptize with the Holy Spirit, and this would be included in that. One of the most wonderful benefits and blessings that follow with the Holy Spirit in our heart is that we become conscious of the living Lord Jesus Christ.

An anointing is something given to a person like oil poured on one's head in an anointing ceremony. It is something given to a person from God, and it will stay with him as long as he lives. He will be conscious of the presence of the living Lord Jesus Christ, and "ye need not that any man teach you" because anyone who attempts to teach him will be compared to Christ. If any man teaches in agreement with Christ, he will be acceptable; if he does not teach in agreement with Christ, he will not be acceptable. So it does not make so much difference what any human being may say, since "the same anointing teacheth you of all things. . . ."

In the fourteenth chapter of John's Gospel, there is the promise that the Holy Spirit when He came would teach believers all things. The function of the Holy Spirit is to show the things of Christ to believers. Believers learn the truth, and even as it is taught, they shall abide in Christ. No one can take that away from them. That will be the thing that will enable believers to tell whether what they hear is right or wrong.

Then John goes on to say: "And now, little children, abide in him." That is, "Turn yourself over willingly to this fellowship with the Lord." The Holy Spirit will make believers conscious of Christ's presence and will incline them in mind and heart to want to walk with Him, that "when he shall appear, we may have confidence, and not be ashamed before him at his coming" (v. 28).

This may refer to the coming of the Lord Jesus Christ in judgment. I sometimes think it might also refer to coming into His presence at any time, especially in some given situation, perhaps in a special crisis when the believer is in trouble, wondering what to do. Christ can come to the believer in such a way that His Holy Spirit can show the believer the things of Christ any time. Then John says the believer can have confidence and not be ashamed before Him at His coming. In other words, if the believer keeps the conscious presence of the Lord Jesus Christ in his heart, he need not be afraid of what decisions or judgments he may be led to make.

As far as knowing right from wrong, and whether he should go this way or that, if one is conscious of the things of the Lord Jesus Christ, that will be adequate; the Lord will take care of him. John says one more thing: "If ye know that he is righteous, ye know that every one that doeth righteousness is born of him." This is the measuring stick. The believer will know perfectly well how it was with the Lord Jesus Christ, and anyone who comes and talks to him, if he is like that, is all right; but if he is not like that, he is not all right with the believer. The believer knows that Christ is righteous because of the way He lived, and that is the way any obedient person should live in the presence of God.

The believer should ask himself what the Lord Jesus did inasmuch as He was righteous. We know that the word *righteous* is an adjective that means that everything He does is right. What would right be? The believer who knows Scripture will know that means a person will do everything in line with the will of God. What would that be? As far as the Lord Jesus is concerned, He had reverence for His Father, in fact He worshiped His Father. He took time to pray, sometimes spending an entire night in prayer. He always obeyed and trusted His Father in everything. He handled the Scriptures reverently. He said that not "one jot or one tittle [would] in no wise pass from the law, till all be fulfilled" (Matt. 5:18). Whenever I hear anything said that honors the Scripture and takes Scripture as the Word of God, I know that person is talking the way the Lord Jesus Christ talked; however, if a person suggests that the Bible doesn't mean what it says, that it has mistakes in it, then I know I am listening to someone who is not like the Lord Jesus Christ.

This is what John means; this is the anointing that I have within that will enable me to judge anyone I hear. Now think how Jesus dealt with men. He showed respect; He even respected Pilate in the courtroom. He was considerate of people, and He was charitable to the poor. If someone is not kind to other people and does not respect authority, then he is not like Jesus Christ.

And what should be our attitude toward the world? John had said earlier, "Love not the world." Jesus Christ did not love the world. He lived in this world, but He never gave Himself over to it. Whatever a person may be doing or saying, if he is acting the way we know the Lord Jesus would act, we have reason to believe that the Holy Spirit of God is working in him. Otherwise we know that He is not. This is what John means here.

Chapter 12

BECOMING A BELIEVER IS LIKE
RECEIVING A GIFT

Do you realize that becoming a believer is something you receive? that it is a gift?

In the first two verses of 1 John 3 we will investigate the matter of becoming a believer. Many people think that becoming a believer is a graduation experience, and that one prepares himself for some time until he reaches a certain level of performance — then he would be good enough to be a believer. That may sound like a proper way of approach, but it is not true. Believing begins with receiving an endowment from God. We do not strive to qualify to become believers; He receives us. As a matter of fact, we read that "as many as received him, to them gave he power to become the sons of God" (John 1:12). Then, having been given the blessing of actually being children of God, we rejoice, and we wish to please Him who is our Benefactor.

> Behold, what manner of love the Father hath bestowed upon us, that we should be called the sons of God (1 John 3:1).

We have already talked about love, and we will speak about it more as we study 1 John. Love is an action verb; it is doing something for the welfare of another person. The common idea of love's being an emotion — something you feel inside — is not the biblical use of the word *love*. When we consider here the "manner of love the Father hath bestowed upon us," we should think of the way God has acted toward us. His love took the form of action.

Now look at the word *Father*. I draw your attention to it to note that John does not here say "God." He is not referring here to what manner of love God the Creator has bestowed upon all mankind. It is the love of the "Father," the Father of Jesus Christ who hath bestowed upon us who believe in His Son that we should be called the sons of God, even as Jesus was the only begotten Son of God. In the remainder of the verse John says, "Therefore the world knoweth us not, because it knew him not." This word *therefore* does not point backwards to what God did before in that verse but points forward to what is following. "Therefore [for this reason] the world knoweth us not, [the reason is] because it knew him not" (1 John 3:1).

Let us look more closely at this. "Behold, what manner of love. . . ." Consider what God has done for us. "The Father [of Jesus Christ, the Father of all who put their trust in Him] hath bestowed upon us [has given to us. We did not earn it; this is not wages], that we should be called the sons of God." When John says we should be called the sons of God, he means much more than that this will be our name. This is not a name tag that is hung on; this word *called* has in it the idea that He calls and we respond in obedience. It is not even a label put on us as the finished product. He does not call us the sons of God in the sense that we are perfect and complete. This is the designation of a relationship to which we are called in Christ Jesus . . . "that we should be called [called into the being of] the sons of God."

Paul speaks of himself "called an apostle." This does not mean that someone put that name tag on him, and called him an apostle in that sense, but "called of God." Paul was given a call that required obedience; he was given a challenge, an invitation, an urgent exhortation — a call to be an apostle. When Paul writes to believers, he sometimes speaks about them as being "called saints." This does not mean just the name "saint" put on them, but *called* to be saints. That we should be called to be the sons of God. We can properly insert this and read, "Behold, what manner of love the Father hath bestowed upon us, that we should be called to be the sons of God:

therefore the world knoweth us not, because it knew him not," which is a way of saying that for the same reasons the world did not appreciate Jesus Christ, they will not appreciate us.

Here is a crucial point in the experience of a believer. It is important that you do not think of yourself in the sight of God the way the world thinks of you; but that you think of yourself the way God speaks of you. If you were to act the way the world considers you, it would appear that you do not belong to God; but if you will act in His way, you will know that you do belong to Him.

Now look at the second verse: "Beloved, now are we the sons of God." The word *beloved* tells us that we are the fortunate ones, those who have received the blessing of God, and the word *now* is always the word of the Holy Spirit.

> Beloved, now are we the sons of God, and it doth not yet appear what we shall be: but we know that, when he shall appear, we shall be like him; for we shall see him as he is (1 John 3:2).

This brings to our minds another passage in Scripture:

> But we all, with open face beholding as in a glass the glory of the Lord, are changed into the same image from glory to glory, even as by the Spirit of the Lord (2 Cor. 3:18).

We can be sure we will be like Him because we will see Him in the reality of His being.

As we think about the Lord Jesus Christ and focus our attention on Him, by the blessing of God and of the Holy Spirit, God will actually transform us into the likeness of the Lord Jesus Christ. This is all ahead of us, however. In this matter of becoming believers, and because we are believers, we go on living it out. I am reminded, for instance, of the time when I first joined the Canadian army in the First World War. When I went into the recruiting office to sign up as a volunteer, they filled out all of the blanks and I signed my name. When I signed my name, I became a soldier and began to draw pay from that day on. A year afterwards I knew much more about soldiering, but I wasn't any more of a soldier. I was a soldier when I signed my name on the paper.

We can also think in terms of people getting married. When the preacher says, "I pronounce you husband and wife," they are legally husband and wife; and from that moment they will become more and more involved in each other. Likewise, when I become one of God's children it is not a position I earn; it is a position that I enter into. After I am in this position I look up into God's face, knowing that I came into this position because He called me. I am received because Christ Jesus died for me; I am forgiven for His sake.

Seeing the Lord Jesus as He is may refer to that ultimate time when He will be revealed from heaven, and everything on earth will be finished, so to speak. He will come in power and glory. While I am in this world, I should worship the Lord Jesus Christ, think about Him, focus my attention upon Him, and in that way grow in grace and knowledge, becoming more like Him all the time.

Chapter 13

SALVATION, A PRECIOUS POSSESSION

Do you think that if a person is a believer and belongs to God it will mean that he can be careless in his life, that he will sin and just do anything he wants to do?

We have noticed in the first two verses of the third chapter that John makes the strong point that a believer's relationship to God is something given to him; he does not earn it. Now John takes up this question, Is this likely to cause a man to become careless or to take advantage of God? In other words, wouldn't it be better for a teacher to hold out, to threaten the believer by saying he might not make it? Do you think you would be a better person if kept in the dark, not knowing for sure? Do you think you would try harder that way?

I wonder if you realize that such a procedure would affect you as a human being, but that is not the way God works with you in spiritual matters. When I speak of its effect on you as a human being, I mean that the more scared you may be, the harder you will try; but you would not be able to make it anyway. You would not have within you naturally the power necessary to do the will of God. Everything you did would be done in some way to satisfy self. John points out that no one ever need worry about the effect in the soul when one knows he is confident in his relationship with God. Someone will say, "Wouldn't that make a man careless, as if he didn't have to strive any more?" And the answer to that is that we need only remember what belonging to Him means. When you receive Jesus Christ in faith, something happens to you. According to

Scripture you are "born again"; and now, because you are so received and have been born again, there is no longer any urgency to strive to qualify. You have been accepted.

> But as many as received him, to them gave he power to become the sons of God (John 1:12).

This is where believers are; but does this mean that now they will be careless? What this actually means could be described like this: Suppose I had been in a boat which sank, and I have been thrown into the ocean. I cannot swim well, but I swim as long as I can, trying to hold myself above water long enough for people to rescue me. When I am rescued, they put me in a lifeboat. What John is saying here is that I do not go on swimming. I am in the lifeboat and I am safe.

Does that mean that I will be careless or unappreciative? As I was naturally in my sin, it would be my disposition to be lazy and careless. But when I become a believer in the Lord Jesus Christ and receive Him as my Savior, God does something to me. Something happens in me. Christ Himself comes into my heart, and my whole inner disposition is changed to where I want to obey God. I want to please Him.

Every believer has the hope of seeing Jesus Christ and the hope of being transformed in His presence.

> Beloved, now are we the sons of God, and it doth not yet appear what we shall be: but we know that, when he shall appear, we shall be like him; for we shall see him as he is. And every man that hath this hope in him purifieth himself, even as he is pure (1 John 3:2,3).

John goes on to point out, "Whosoever committeth sin transgresseth also the law: for sin is the transgression of the law" (v. 4). If a person is sinning, he is going against the nature of God. The word *law* here refers to the law of God, which is the nature of God, His way of doing things. If a person is committing sin, he is not obeying God.

> And ye know that he was manifested to take away our sins; and in him is no sin (1 John 3:5).

When we receive Christ Jesus as our Savior, the plan is to loose us from our sin. The nature of God was in Jesus of Nazareth, so there was no sin in Him. "Whosoever abideth in him sinneth not . . ." (1 John 3:6). In the fifteenth chapter of John's Gospel, Jesus said:

> I am the vine, ye are the branches: He that abideth in me, and I in him, the same bringeth forth much fruit: for without me ye can do nothing (John 15:5).

The person who abides in the Lord Jesus Christ, committing himself totally to Him to live and have fellowship with Him, is not practicing sin. "Sinneth not" means it will not be his custom to do the wrong thing.

> Whosoever abideth in him sinneth not: whosoever sinneth hath not seen him, neither known him (1 John 3:6).

The latter part of that statement may seem rather flat, but John wants to make it obvious. He is saying that if a person has received Jesus Christ into his heart, he will be led in the way of obedience. And if a person is not led in that way, but is practicing sin in doing selfish things, then he has no relationship with the Lord Jesus Christ. To make it as simple as possible, let's suppose Jesus is walking north. If I am walking with Him, which way am I going? If I am walking north, I am certainly not walking south. This is what John is saying. Whoever is in the Lord, and has the Lord in him, sinneth not. That means he is not practicing sin. He may fall into it, but it is not his custom; because, having received Jesus Christ into his heart, he now has Christ the hope of glory in him. Christ's purpose is to do the will of His Father, and Christ's general attitude toward sin is to repudiate it; and if the Lord Jesus is in a person and leading him, he will be moved inwardly to repudiate sin.

John is emphasizing this fact so that believers need not be confused or worried. They will discover that if they really do belong to the Lord, they will be inwardly led to obey Him. This will follow not because they want to belong in order to qualify, but because they already do belong to Him. Hope in the Lord Jesus Christ means that the soul is purified from sin; and "every man that hath this hope in him," the expectation of seeing Jesus Christ, has this hope, because it is based upon the fact that he belongs to Him now. And what does belonging to Him mean? It means He has my hand in His, so that where He goes, I go; what He does, I do. If I am abiding in Him and going in the way He goes, when He goes north, I go north; when He goes south, I go south; and when He goes east, I go east. What He does in obedience to God, I will be doing in obedience to God.

Chapter 14

HAVING GRACE IN THE HEART

When is a man a thief? Must a man steal in order to be a thief? What was he before he stole? Do you think he was honest? Would an honest man steal?

In this letter John is talking about the meaning of true spiritual experience. He does so because he wants believers to rejoice in their faith. He wants them to have fellowship with each other and with the Lord, and to be filled with joy. It would seem that the more one understands about his relationship with the Lord, the more effective it will be, and therefore the more joy he will have. We have been considering the matter of becoming a child of God, of how one becomes a believer by receiving the Lord Jesus Christ as Savior, and of how a person is, from the beginning, one of His, belonging to Him. This is not true for everyone on the face of the earth. It is true for "whosoever believeth."

Now with reference to spiritual matters that have to do with the experience of a believer it is easy to be deceived and to get wrong ideas, because everything that pertains to God and the soul is invisible. "No man hath seen God at any time," and no one has seen the soul. Everything that has to do with spiritual experience refers to something which is not seen, and for this reason believers become uncertain. This is especially the case when people come along with strange ideas and make them sound plausible. Then believers are inclined to turn in all directions, wondering who might possibly be right.

John has this peril in mind and it is refreshing to hear him warn so plainly:

> Little children, let no man deceive you: he that doeth
> righteousness is righteous, even as he is righteous (1 John
> 3:7).

It sounds simple, doesn't it? But right here is something subtle
and profound. John is saying that righteous living comes out of
a righteous heart. A person does not do the right thing in order
to become a child of God; a person becomes a believer in order
that he might do the right thing. The believer is not righteous
because he is practicing righteousness. Righteousness comes
by faith, as Abraham found out. It is by believing in God and
trusting in Him that the soul becomes righteous. God receives
the believer and accepts him, the believer then begins doing
the right thing with the guidance and help of God. If a person
wants to be a child of God, the place to start is by being born
again. And he can be born again just the way a baby is born,
with no effort on his part. He receives the Lord Jesus Christ as
his Savior and "as many as received him, to them gave he
power to become the sons of God, even to them that believe on
his name" (John 1:12).

Suppose I raise the same question I asked at the beginning of
this chapter: When is a man a thief? There are some people
who have been given that label, and some people actually are
thieves. For a long time in my life I would have said a man is a
thief when he steals, and not until he steals. But now I ask you,
What is he before he steals? If you tell me he is an honest man, I
will point out that if he had been an honest man, he would not
have stolen. Think about that. If a man is honest before he
steals, he will never steal. Why does he steal? Because he is a
thief. He took the first chance to steal because he had that
nature and that disposition. "He that doeth righteousness is
righteous" before he starts working, because he is righteous.
He is righteous in his conduct even as he is righteous in his
heart.

The Lord Jesus is the one perfectly righteous Person. He is
the "Righteous Servant" mentioned in the Old Testament, the
one who is perfect in the sight of God. Jesus of Nazareth did the
Father's will in every way. When I become a believer, I

receive Jesus Christ as my Lord and Savior, and He shares His righteousness with me; it will be revealed in my conduct because I will want to do the right thing. Only a child of God will walk in His ways; natural men do not want to.

> He that committeth sin is of the devil; for the devil sinneth from the beginning. For this purpose the Son of God was manifested, that he might destroy the works of the devil" (1 John 3:8).

When we see a person who is sinning, we know he is not being led by the Lord Jesus Christ, because "He was made in all points like as we are yet without sin." He lived a perfect life. The person practicing wrongdoing is being led by the same one who led Eve and Adam into sin, that is, Satan. He is the author of sin from the very first. When a person is doing right toward God, he works with God and obeys Him. In doing right toward my fellowman, I consider him and appreciate him; if he is above me, I honor him; and if he is below me, I act with charity toward him. In doing right toward the world, I deny the world. I will not let it gain dominion over me.

John states plainly that whoever commits sin — the person who practices wrongdoing — is of the devil. He gets his inspiration from the devil, who sinneth from the beginning. For this purpose the Son of God was manifested, that He might destroy the works of the devil. The devil wants to approach me and work with me by appealing to my flesh, my imagination, and my vanity. The Lord Jesus Christ took on the form of flesh; He took that flesh to the cross and crucified it so that it would be dead. He had that killed in which Satan would work. He destroyed the works of Satan, because the flesh in which Satan would operate is reckoned dead.

> Whosoever is born of God doth not commit sin; for his seed remaineth in him: and he cannot sin, because he is born of God (1 John 3:9).

Such a person does not practice sin. The person who is born of God has God as Father and is the child of God; in the same way as Jesus Christ, he does not practice sin. Since God cannot sin, that which is born of Him in me cannot sin; that is to say, it does not willingly and willfully turn away from God — this new thing I have in me is of God. John is arguing that if you see me sinning, you will know it is not because Christ is in me; it is because Satan is operative in my flesh. My deliverance from that comes if I reckon the flesh dead through Christ Jesus; then Satan cannot operate in me. In that way Christ Jesus would have destroyed the works of the devil.

> In this the children of God are manifest, and the children of the devil: whosoever doeth not righteousness is not of God, neither he that loveth not his brother. For this is the message that ye heard from the beginning, that we should love one another. Not as Cain, who was of that wicked one, and slew his brother . . . (1 John 3:10–12).

After John had discussed the whole matter of doing righteously, he brings all this out to a specific illustration, with reference to love toward a brother.

Chapter 15

THE TEST OF A BELIEVER

Is there any way a person can know for sure that he is a child of God, that he belongs to the Lord?

In this study you may find it somewhat difficult to keep in mind what John is pointing toward. You will have to remember that John is talking about the nature of spiritual life and experience. That is not easy to see because spiritual life and experience concern the soul, the spirit, and God. All three are invisible; so everything we are talking about in spiritual living is something unseen, yet very real. It is wonderful for a person to know for sure that he is a child of God; however, sometimes things happen to make him question whether he is or not.

There may be times when he meets people who say strange and different things, and in his confusion he can actually begin to doubt. Then in his doubt he becomes weak; and when he becomes weak, he does not have the blessing. When he does not have the blessing, he does not have the joy, and so there is no thanksgiving; he simply does not have the life that he could have in Jesus Christ.

John has written his Epistle so believers could learn more about this. He is primarily concerned that believers understand the truth of spiritual living which is made possible in Jesus Christ. He uses certain specific illustrations to demonstrate what he has in mind. We noticed here in the third chapter how he has been emphasizing the fact that the believing person does the right thing because the Lord Jesus Christ does the right thing, and the believing person has the Spirit in him, moving him to do the right thing. John has made the point in this third chapter that believers are now the sons of God; believing people are already received as the children of God. It is not something they earn; it is something given to them. They can be assured of this as they watch their own conduct.

John now discusses loving the brethren, because the Son of God came to do things for man. Since He came to give His life for men and His Spirit is in me, I ought to do things for others naturally. Jesus Christ came to do the will of God. If I am in Christ, then I want to do the will of God. So John says plainly:

> We know that we have passed from death unto life, because we love the brethren (1 John 3:14).

That is to say, believers can know that they have actually become new creatures in Christ Jesus, that God is actually living in them, and that they have passed out of the state of death in sins into the state of life with Christ, when they love the brethren. The Lord Jesus Christ came to love the brethren; and when believers are in Him and He in them, they too will love the brethren.

> He that loveth not his brother abideth in death (1 John 3:14).

That is putting the other side of it clearly. Loving a brother does not mean the believer approves him or that he likes him. It means that he is interested in his brother's welfare, as the Good Samaritan was interested in the man in the ditch. The person who has no interest in the welfare of others is actually living the way he lived as an unbeliever, as a human being in sin.

> Whosoever hateth his brother is a murderer (1 John 3:15).

There are two strong words in this verse, and it is difficult to grasp them in our ordinary use of language. One is *hate*. Earlier we spoke of John's using a number of words to refer to the life that is in God. He says God is light; therefore, darkness is being without God. Again, God is life, and those who have Him have life; while those who do not have Him are condemned to death. Now, when there is no love, there is hate.

John does not mean overt malice or anger, or necessarily any sort of hostile action against a man. He simply means that one person does not love the other. It is dark in the soul as far as the other man is concerned. John calls that murder. Why? Because if another man is in need, for example, if he were drowning and I walk away leaving him to drown, I am actually condemning him to death.

> Hereby perceive we the love of God, because he laid down his life for us (1 John 3:16).

We say that God loves us. Does that mean that He thinks we are nice? No. Does it mean that He thinks we are good? That is not true. But He laid down His life for us anyway. So John says believers ought also to lay down their lives for the brethren, if they belong to Him. In verse 17 he uses a practical illustration:

> But whoso hath this world's good, and seeth his brother have need, and shutteth up his bowels of compassion from him, how dwelleth the love of God in him? (1 John 3:17).

If God is in a person, will that person let another man starve while he himself has food? How could that be called the love of God? To John that would be ridiculous, because God takes of His own and gives to us.

> My little children, let us not love in word, neither in tongue; but in deed and in truth. And hereby we know that we are of the truth, and shall assure our hearts before him (1 John 3:18,19).

When love is put into action, and believers live and do for other people, they have the evidence that they really do belong to Him, and they can be confident before Him.

So John has pressed this point home that the matter of loving the brethren means actually helping others, doing things for them, and all this is based on the fact that this is what God would do. If a person receives Jesus Christ as Savior and opens his heart to His Holy Spirit, the Holy Spirit will move him to act in certain ways. He will keep God's Word; he will listen to Him and be obedient. He will help his fellowman. If he is in sorrow and distress, he will comfort him. He will put himself out on behalf of the other person not because he is good, but because the Lord Jesus Christ is in him moving him to do these things. When that happens he has the evidence that he belongs to God. If he really will reach out to other people in their need, the evidence is that God is actually working in him and he belongs to God as His child.

Chapter 16

THE CONDUCT OF A BELIEVER

The spiritual experience of the believer is often clouded with doubt — not doubt about God or Christ or the gospel, but doubt about himself. A person can easily become uncertain as to whether he really belongs to God, and such doubt hinders his fellowship and hampers his service. Above all, it stifles his praying. He just does not feel good in the presence of God if he is not sure that he belongs. When he prays, he has no real confidence that God will hear him, because he feels unfit. This unfit feeling in his heart is valid; it is legitimate. But to think that this will then disqualify him is a mistake. As a matter of fact, this is the very condition that God is looking to help.

In the Bible we read: "A broken and a contrite heart, O God, thou wilt not despise" (Ps. 51:17). Again, the Scripture records that God seeks those of a humble spirit and He appreciates them. So it is natural for a person who is honest and not proud to be realistic about himself. It is natural for him to be discouraged as he sees his faults. The apostle Paul said, "I know that in me [that is, in my flesh] dwelleth no good thing" (Rom. 7:18). The fact that a person feels unfit and unworthy is sound. It has its basis in actual fact.

There is a further kind of doubt as to whether or not God will be gracious, whether or not God will receive him. A person could doubt Jesus' being the Son of God: Was He really born of a virgin? Was He actually conceived of the Holy Spirit? A person can have doubt about Jesus' being the Christ: Is He the only way a person can come to God? Is He right when He says,

"I am the way, the truth, and the life: no man cometh unto the Father, but by me" (John 14:6)? A person can also doubt his own acceptance by God. A person may feel that he has been in God's favor, heard the truth about God, and been ready to believe that Christ actually lived and died the way it is written; but he may yet doubt that he has accepted Christ as his Savior.

Every kind of doubt yields to proof when it is presented in concrete events. As far as God is concerned, a person may think many different things about God, but when we look at nature, "The heavens declare the glory of God; and the firmament showeth his handiwork" (Ps. 19:1). If a person were to recognize the hand of God in daily affairs, he would know about God. The same is true about Jesus Christ. One might wonder about the virgin birth, but when he studies the life of Jesus of Nazareth and His death and everything that has happened since then, and considers all the people the gospel has blessed, he is not surprised that the Son of God came into the world in the way it is written that He did. The same is true with reference to Jesus' being the Christ. If someone were to wonder if the life of Jesus of Nazareth was God's idea of living, he need only think of the effect Christ has had in the world during these almost two thousand years, and what has happened to mankind under the inspiration and the guidance of the Christian gospel — his doubts will fade away.

My doubt as to my own personal integrity, as to whether or not I am really a believer, and as to whether I have done what I have said I have done is difficult to remove because it is so personal. I would say for anyone who is interested in himself, if he has the problem in his own heart and would concede everything about the Bible and everything about God and Jesus Christ and the gospel but still, deep within he has this uneasiness or doubt as to whether or not he really belongs, I would suggest that he is looking in the wrong direction. He is looking at himself, and preoccupation with self can be very disturbing. If he looks at himself, he will lose confidence. It is better to look into the face of God. He should turn his mind upward; he should look into the face of God and the Lord Jesus. The Bible tells us: "Look unto me, and be ye saved, all the ends of the earth" (Isa. 45:22).

Now John deals with this whole problem of confidence in our relationship with God.

> For if our heart condemn us, God is greater than our heart, and knoweth all things (1 John 3:20).

John takes into account that there will be some who will feel self-condemned, and he would simply say, "God is greater than our heart, and knoweth all things." I might not know everything that is in my own heart, nor the full meaning of all. Paul says, "I judge not my own self." We cannot judge ourselves. We cannot see inside our own hearts as God does; and if He says He will forgive, we can believe Him. When God says whosoever will may come, believe that Word, and you can come.

> Beloved, if our heart condemn us not, then have we confidence toward God. And whatsoever we ask, we receive of him, because we keep his commandments, and do those things that are pleasing in his sight (1 John 3:21,22).

This confidence is important because it leads to power in prayer. If a believer feels that he belongs, he can ask God. If he does not feel that he belongs and is uncertain about it at all, then he will not be inclined to trust and to ask God. He will feel that perhaps he shouldn't. As we put verses 21 and 22 together, we see that if our hearts do not condemn us, then we have confidence toward God.

Under what conditions would our hearts not condemn us? When could I not have this inner feeling of unfitness? If I kept His commandments, if I were obedient and listened to Him, and if I would do those things that are pleasing in His sight, then my heart would not condemn me and I would have confidence in prayer. Effective confidence in praying is grounded in our activating our response to Him and in our actually doing what He wants us to do — keeping His commandments. If we practice obedience in conduct, then we can pray with confidence.

What is His commandment?

> And this is his commandment, That we should believe on
> the name of his Son Jesus Christ, and love one another, as
> he gave us commandment (1 John 3:23).

In those two statements can be seen again the two directions of
the two great commandments. Remember how Jesus said the
first commandment is: "Thou shalt love the Lord thy God. . . .
And the second is like unto it, Thou shalt love thy neighbour as
thyself" (Matt. 22:37,39). They are both here. His will is quite
clear as far as believers are concerned.

The life of God in Jesus that led Him to self-denial and
brought Him to the cross is God's way of dealing with this
world. Because it is God's way, and in that sense is approved
and offered to the whole world, the name of Christ is used
there. He is the Anointed One. If a person believes on the
name of God's Son, Jesus Christ, he receives Jesus as his Savior
and Lord, and he follows Him. He walks with Him. He lets His
Spirit control his heart. If he does this, he will pass through the
experience of dying unto sin and being raised from the dead by
the power of God; and this is Christ's way. This is the experience of the believer.

The first requirement is: Thou shalt believe on the name of
His Son Jesus Christ. The second is: Love one another as He
gave us commandment.

> And he that keepeth his commandments dwelleth in him,
> and he in him . . . (1 John 3:24a).

This is John's basic thrust. The believer can know for sure he is
a child of God if he is obedient in response to the Lord, actually
living in communion with Christ and dwelling in Him.

> . . . And hereby we know that he abideth in us, by the
> Spirit which he hath given us (1 John 3:24b).

This way the believer is inwardly led, inwardly prompted to
obey and to trust God.

Chapter 17

THE BELIEVER'S ATTITUDES

Can a person be really sure that he belongs to God and that he truly does believe?

The fact that many of us feel unworthy has its basis in actual fact. There is a doubt as to whether or not God will be gracious to us and receive us. We can have doubts about Jesus being the Christ. Do you believe He is the only way a person can come to God? Is He right when He says, "I am the way, the truth, and the life: no man cometh unto the Father, but by me" (John 14:6)? We may have doubts about our own acceptance of Him.

It is not peculiar that believers are often confronted with false ideas. These ideas are just as real, just as true, and just as dangerous as any other enemy would be. The first couple on earth, Adam and Eve, were put in the world and given every opportunity to obey God there in the Garden of Eden. They were told to dress it and keep it; they were instructed by God. But Satan came and deceived and tempted them. Satan is still active. He "as a roaring lion, walketh about, seeking whom he may devour" (1 Peter 5:8), even in and around the church. He would like to keep people from believing in the Lord Jesus Christ; and if they do believe in Him, Satan wants to keep them from growing. He seems to be especially active in the church; and of all the things he does in the church, I often think he is nowhere more active than in the matter of interpreting the Bible. There are people teaching the Bible who do not increase our confidence in the Scriptures; in fact, they actually give us reasons to doubt the Bible.

John deals with this in his First Epistle.

> Beloved, believe not every spirit, but try the spirits
> whether they are of God: Because many false prophets are
> gone out into the world (1 John 4:1).

John is telling us not to believe every person who speaks and
brings a message, but to try the messengers and their mes-
sages. Trying them means testing them to see whether they are
of God. What makes a false prophet so dangerous is that he
looks authentic. If a man comes to me and tells me the truth, I
have an appreciation of and respect for that man; but the false
person says that he stands for everything I stand for, whereas in
reality he does not.

Every teaching that is developed from the idea that the Son
of God became incarnate as Jesus of Nazareth — and that His
mode of living showed that He was the Christ, the Son of the
living God — can be trusted.

> Hereby know ye the Spirit of God: Every spirit that
> confesseth that Jesus Christ is come in the flesh is of God
> (1 John 4:2).

This is an assurance that every person who presents a message
which is based on the idea that Jesus Christ is actually from
God, and that He has the truth in Him, is of God. Every spirit
that does not confess that Jesus Christ is come in the flesh is not
of God. This does not mean that such would deny that Jesus of
Nazareth lived. Nor would they deny that He died. What they
do deny is that this Jesus of Nazareth, who lived and died in
Palestine in the city of Jerusalem, is the Son of God.

> And every spirit that confesseth not that Jesus Christ is
> come in the flesh is not of God: and this is that spirit of
> antichrist, whereof ye have heard that it should come; and
> even now already is it in the world (1 John 4:3).

This is the person who claims to belong to God, and tells us that
he teaches the ways of God, but does not base his testimony on
being born again. He may even use Jesus Christ as an example,
but his whole idea would be, "You can do it. Just improve
yourself and you will be all right." He may even say that God is
your Creator and your Judge. But the real question will be, Is
God going to create a new thing in me? Will I be born again into

the family of God? Will God now be my Father as He was the Father of Jesus of Nazareth?

Deceivers do not talk about these things. They actually mislead us and should be considered false teachers. Such messengers were already active in John's time. They were teaching what we would call Christian virtues or ethics, but they did not base their message on the Christian premise that this is Christ in you, the hope of Glory, and that you do these things by the power of God. They would more likely teach that their doctrine is the right way to live, and you ought to follow it. The intimation is that you can if you try.

> Ye are of God, little children, and have overcome them: because greater is he that is in you, than he that is in the world (1 John 4:4).

Christian confidence in facing any of these wrong teachings can be strengthened by remembering that the believer belongs to God. False prophets are those who will teach you that you can live the life of a believer in your own strength, and that any human being can live right with God if he just wants to. Such false teachers are of the world, and because they are of the world, believers have an advantage over them. Believers should realize that they have already won over the error just as they have won over the world as a whole.

> They are of the world: therefore speak they of the world, and the world heareth them (1 John 4:5).

The world listens and understands false teachers because they speak from the world's point of view. They are popular in the public eye because they proceed on natural premises. Often prominent people talk about the gospel from the natural man's point of view, interpreting everything from the human stand-point. Those who are interested find this acceptable because the natural man can understand it; but John would say that though these ideas may be popular, they would not be with real believers. Believers overcome them, because "greater is he that is in you, than he that is in the world."

> We are of God: he that knoweth God heareth us; he that is

not of God heareth not us. Hereby know we the spirit of truth, and the spirit of error (1 John 4:6).

The message of the gospel is received only by those who have received Christ Jesus. We can tell who really belongs to Him because they are the ones who respond when we preach the gospel as it is revealed in Jesus Christ.

Chapter 18

LOVE FOR OTHERS

Do you know the difference between *loving* and *liking?*

Being a child of God is something we need to consider seriously. It is somewhat like having a garden. Anyone who has had a garden of lovely flowers or fine vegetables knows how important it is to work in the garden. As it is with a garden, so it is with one's spiritual life. If you and I are going to grow as believers, we need to study. The more we understand the Bible, the stronger our faith will be, the more we will see God's hand in our affairs, and the greater joy we will have in Him.

When we look at 1 John 4:7, we will find that after John has written everything to this point by way of showing what the real life in Christ is, he now puts his finger on the heart of the matter when he talks about love. I have often said that if I were going to rewrite the English language, I would need about five or six words for *love*, because there are many different ideas expressed by that one word. For now we are just going to try to understand its meaning in the Bible.

The word *love* is not used to indicate sentiment; it is not a feeling, how we feel inside. The word *love* is not even a matter of liking. When we love someone in the New Testament sense, we are not necessarily saying we like him. Of course, it is very easy to love a person we like; in fact, I suspect that in using the word *love*, almost everyone has the idea of "like." If we say we love someone, it nearly always means we like that person. We commonly use it that way when we refer to things. A woman will say, "I just love that coat." She means she likes it very much. Or perhaps someone will say, "I just love my new car," meaning he likes it a great deal. Those are common ways we use the word *love*. But, of course, this is misleading if we examine the New Testament use of the word.

The Bible uses the word *love* as something quite different from the idea of *like*. For instance,

> But God commendeth his love toward us, in that, while we were yet sinners, Christ died for us (Rom. 5:8).

Now we know God does not like sin. He "is angry with the wicked every day" (Ps. 7:11).

Love is used in the Bible mainly as an action word; it is more an adverb than a verb. It has to do more with the direction of our conduct than with what the conduct actually is. Anything you do can show love, yet the same kind of action might also reveal the absence of love. What you do has love in it if you are doing it for other people; but if you do not do it for other people, it does not have love in it. The motive is what counts. Love is the very essence of God's way of doing things. It is important to comprehend this in understanding the life in Christ.

I suppose I should point out right away that the opposite of love is selfishness. Many times we think of hate as being the opposite of love. Actually, hate is the *absence* of love. If you do not love, John would say that you hate.

Think, for example, about what we do with money. If we have money and give it to help others, that is love. If we take this money and spend it on ourselves for personal reasons, that is selfishness. The word *love* is used in the New Testament as seeking the welfare and the happiness of others. We remember the outstanding passage:

> For God so loved the world, that he gave his only begotten Son, that whosoever believeth in him should not perish, but have everlasting life (John 3:16).

John is going to point out that this matter of love is the very essence of God. It is the essence of the whole universe. In other words, fulfillment of being is generally found in usefulness to someone else — in doing for others.

"Beloved, let us love one another [that is, each doing something on behalf of the other's welfare and happiness]: for love is of God [that is where it originated]; and every one that loveth is born of God, and knoweth God" (1 John 4:7). This does not mean that everyone who likes someone else, or everyone who likes certain things and wishes he had them, is of God. "Everyone that loveth" refers to everyone who is active on behalf of others and puts himself out in order that other people may prosper. This person "is born of God and knoweth God." He is being obedient to God because love is God's idea. Natural man's focus is on himself; God's focus is on the other person.

> He that loveth not knoweth not God; for God is love (1 John 4:8).

The person whose life is devoid of this interest in helping other people is not obedient to God. God wants us to be interested in others.

> In this was manifested the love of God toward us, because that God sent his only begotten Son into the world, that we might live through him (1 John 4:9).

So Jesus Christ came into the world to suffer, to die for sinners, to be raised from the dead, and to be taken into the presence of God to intercede on behalf of believers. All of this was done so that believers might live. This is the very nature of God.

> Herein is love, not that we loved God, but that he loved us, and sent his Son to be the propitiation for our sins (1 John 4:10).

We will not get anywhere by telling each other that we should love God, because we do not have the ability on our own to love God. The same is true about loving our fellowman. We may read that we should love our fellowman, but all the time we will have in our hearts a natural desire for self. When it comes to loving our enemies, that is ridiculous. The human, natural way is to defend self against the enemy. Loving our enemies is God's way. "Herein is love" — man did not start this thing. He loved us "and sent his Son to be the propitiation for our sins."

> Beloved, if God so loved us, we ought also to love one
> another (1 John 4:11).

If this is the nature of the gospel that He sent on our behalf, we
ought also to send and to do on behalf of others.

> No man hath seen God at any time. If we love one
> another, God dwelleth in us, and his love is perfected in
> us (1 John 4:12).

When John says that no one has seen God at any time, I
believe this means that no one has seen God so he could imitate
Him or "like" Him. There is nothing about His appearance that
appeals to us, since we cannot even see His appearance. What
happens is that the love of God is shown to us in Jesus Christ.
As we receive Him into our hearts, something happens inside,
and we are inclined toward God. And as we are inclined toward
God and turn toward Him, we want to obey and honor Him.

This is the result of the love of God being operative in us. If
we love one another, God dwelleth in us. He is operative in us
and His love is perfected in us, brought to completion. It bears
fruit in us, and we see that belonging to God is a matter of being
interested in helping other people.

Chapter 19

THE BELIEVER'S DESIRES PROVIDED FOR IN CHRIST

How do believers know that they have the indwelling Holy Spirit of God?

> Hereby know we that we dwell in him, and he in us, because he hath given us of his Spirit (1 John 4:13).

As we have progressed, I hope you have become more and more aware of what John is trying to do. He is explaining all that is involved in the experience of believing so we may enter into it more fully. He wants us to have fellowship with God the Father, with Jesus Christ His Son, and with each other; in this fellowship He knows that we will have joy. Those who study the Bible believe that John is the Apostle of Love, and that seems probable in view of how often John uses the word, especially in this Epistle. However, it would be misleading to think that John was a soft, mild, retiring man. When he speaks of love, he is not speaking about something that is always sweet in its manner, or that is not related to the rugged aspects of life. I often think people believe that a real true child of God is one who does not take active part in anything and just feels kindly toward all people, hoping everything will work out all right.

That picture does not fit John. If you want an idea about the writer of this Epistle, I suggest you think along this line: Have you ever seen a group of people talking about someone in trouble, someone in an unfortunate situation? They express their sympathy and then one person will usually start to do something about helping the victim. John was that type of person. He felt that talk amounts to something only if you act, and I am inclined to say he was one who was not so strong on "talk" as he was on "walk." John's premise was that the life of God operating in a believer will move that believer to act in line with the will of God. That will lead him toward being obedient to the guidance of God in his daily life and being thoughtful of his fellowman.

We would call this moving that takes place in a man the work of the Holy Spirit.

> Hereby know we that we dwell in him, and he in us, because he hath given us of his Spirit (1 John 4:13).

This is a way of saying simply: we can be assured that we know Him or that we dwell in Him, which is to say we abide in Him. You will remember in the Gospel of John, chapter 15, we have the expression "abide in me and I in you." The word *abide* in John's Gospel and this word *dwell* in John's First Epistle are the same word. We have the indwelling Holy Spirit of God. How do we know that? We are reminded of the things of the Lord Jesus Christ, and we are moved in response to that. When the reality of the Lord Jesus Christ is brought to mind over and over again, that is the work of the Holy Spirit.

The Holy Spirit does not speak of Himself, and since He does not have a body, we cannot see Him. We cannot feel Him as if He were a wind or an electric current or anything of that nature, but we can recognize His work. His work in the believer will be operative when we think about Jesus Christ. So John says here we can know for sure that we have a real relationship with Jesus Christ when His Spirit is moving in us.

> And we have seen and do testify that the Father sent the Son to be the Saviour of the world (1 John 4:14).

This is a simple, straightforward statement, and John can make it undoubtedly because the Holy Spirit is working in him. After all, John saw Jesus of Nazareth in person; he saw Him in the Resurrection. We read, "The Father hath sent the Son to be the Saviour of the world." When Jesus of Nazareth was born, He was born of God; He was conceived by the Holy Spirit. God gave life to His child in Mary, and Jesus of Nazareth is the only begotten Son of God who came to be the Savior of the world.

When we speak of the Savior of the world, we think about Jesus Christ dying for our sins and being raised from the dead for our justification. Something happened at Calvary and the Resurrection, which makes it possible for anyone on earth to be saved. There is no indication that He is going to improve this world. Actually, this world will end just about like the husk of wheat when the plant grows out of the kernel, or like the old potato when the plant grows out of the portion of the potato that was put into the ground. This world is not permanent. The world we see is temporal, and this is not the world that the Lord Jesus Christ came to save. He came to save people out of the world; but in the sense that He came into this world to perform His salvation work, we call Him the Savior of the world, that is, of all mankind.

> Whosoever shall confess that Jesus is the Son of God, God dwelleth in him, and he in God (1 John 4:15).

When we say "confess," we mean the believer is able to see and to understand that Jesus in the Incarnation is truly the Son of God, that the life of God came here to be in human form in that Person.

> And we have known and believed the love that God hath to us. God is love; and he that dwelleth in love dwelleth in God, and God in him (1 John 4:16).

John said at one time, "God is light," and at another time he said, "God is life"; but here he says, "God is love." This is characteristic of God. When we think about God, the Creator of the heavens and the earth and the Keeper of man, we are to think about Someone who acts on behalf of people. He dwelleth in love.

If a person is dwelling in love, he will be obedient and reverent toward God. He that dwelleth in love is not thinking of himself — he is thinking about his relationship with others: with God, with man, and with the world. Remember how John wrote "love not the world"? A man who dwells in love will deny himself, and his attitude toward God is one of reverence;

toward man, one of consideration. Any such person dwelleth in God; that is to say, he is actually being conscious of his relationship with God and trusting in Him. I think one reason John could express it so plainly is because if it were not for God, no one would be like that. No ordinary human being would have this disposition, and John is anxious for us to understand that the love of God actually moves us to be interested in the welfare of God, in honoring Him and worshiping Him; in the welfare of man by helping him; and the welfare of the soul by denying the flesh.

This would be a person who is dwelling in God, the way a branch dwells in the vine, and God dwells in him like the life of the vine is in the branch. This brings out the idea that love actually operates in those who belong to God. John wants us to know this, and it is his great emphasis.

Chapter 20

LOVE DELIVERS THE SOUL FROM FEAR

Do you think it is possible for a person to have complete freedom from any fear of future judgment?

No one thinks seriously of facing God without some feeling of self-consciousness. When I think about facing God, or when I consider the fact that He sees me even now every hour of the day, I wonder what He thinks of me. When I have done something questionable, I wonder afterwards how my performance will rate in His estimation. For many people, such a feeling may be one of guilt, which then leads to fear — fear of coming judgment or punishment of some sort. This sort of fear would doubtless dim the hope of heaven. I am distressed when I think of someone who believes in God and in heaven, but who also thinks that between here and there he has to pass through some sort of examination, with some sort of punishment or suffering because of the wrong he has done.

Such an idea is not in the gospel, and John has written his Epistle to deliver us from such an error. He has pointed out how we may have confidence — how we may be sure we will be acceptable in the sight of God.

> Herein is our love made perfect, that we may have boldness in the day of judgment: because as he is, so are we in this world (1 John 4:17).

The way that reads in the version above is just a bit misleading. When it says "herein," it is not referring to what comes later in that verse, but to everything John has been saying. John is emphasizing something that is true in this whole relationship with God, where the life of God is activated in us by the Holy Spirit, when God Himself will work in us to do His will, and is moving us by the Holy Spirit to do His will, to obey Him, and to help others. "Herein is our love made perfect" — in all John has said up to this point, our response to God is brought to its fulfillment through this inward operation of God working in us. In this mutual communion we trust in God and He is gracious to us. We walk with Him as He walks with us. The love of God generates love in us which moves us into action: we keep His commandments, we listen to Him in obedience, we love the brethren, and we do the things He wants us to do for others. This relationship makes possible the completion of love in each of us. This is what is meant by "our love made perfect," and we may therefore have boldness in the day of judgment — we need not be afraid.

You and I may be imperfect; we may stumble as we walk along; but I can tell you this: if from the bottom of your heart you want to be well-pleasing in the sight of God, that is just exactly what Jesus desired, and He did it perfectly. We may do it imperfectly, but God looks on the heart. God accepts it in the way we want it to be. If we have received His love in Christ Jesus, if we have appreciated what God has done for us in His Son, and if we have yielded ourselves to Him and received Jesus Christ as our Savior, the love of God working in us will move us to obey and honor Him, and we will seek to help other people. We will love the brethren, and we will never be afraid of judgment.

> There is no fear in love; but perfect love casteth out fear: because fear hath torment. He that feareth is not made perfect in love (1 John 4:18).

This is a specific observation in which John is saying that when a person is moved from within by the Holy Spirit to seek the will of God and the welfare of others, that individual has no apprehension of unfavorable judgment, nor will he feel guilt. When it says "but perfect love casteth out fear," it does not mean that this is true when you love people all the time, and that you never have a disagreeable thought about them. This "perfect love" does not mean that you are filled with a feeling of good will toward all men all of the time in the fullest sense; it is "perfect" in the sense that it is love that has brought forth action. As John points out in this Epistle, perfect love is that which has been *perfected* in conduct. You have loved God, and you then seek to obey Him. Love that comes to the point where it tries to obey God and to help our fellowman will cast out any feeling of guilt.

A life in which the love of God operates to the keeping of His Word will actually remove guilt from the consciousness because fear has torment. A life in which the love of God, through the coming of the Son of God into the heart, that is moving the believer into fellowship with the Father is marked with joy. Such joy will expel any feeling of uneasy guilt which may have been a hangover from your past. Ordinarily any average human being has a feeling of guilt, of coming judgment, in the presence of God. He should have. He has done wrong and he knows that "the soul that sinneth, it shall die" and that "God is of purer eyes than to behold evil." In thinking of my own past conduct, I would have reason to think that God would judge me; but I believe in the Lord Jesus Christ and I know He has forgiven me. Since He has forgiven my sins, nothing of the past will be held against me.

This leaves only the present. If I truly want to obey God, if I want to listen to Him and help my fellowman, I will not have any guilt feelings. John emphasizes this by saying, "He that feareth is not made perfect in love." Anyone who has guilt feelings is a person who has not been moved into such obedience to God and such love for other people, because if he had, that would have promoted communion and fellowship with the Father. Such a believer would have joy instead of guilt.

We love him, because he first loved us (1 John 4:19).

This is just a reminder John slips in here, so that we will remember we do not have to start this process. We should remember that God started it, and we are invited to receive it. God has already sent His Son into the world for us, and if we will receive Him, we will not be able to refrain from turning and responding to Him.

> If a man say, I love God, and hateth his brother, he is a liar: for he that loveth not his brother whom he hath seen, how can he love God whom he hath not seen? And this commandment have we from him, That he who loveth God love his brother also (1 John 4:20,21).

I think these two verses are here largely as repetition for emphasis. It is a case of saying, "There is no reason to doubt that my loving of God, my being obedient to Him, is actually primary. You cannot tell by looking at me whether I want to obey God, but my loving the brethren indicates that I do. If I really want to obey God, He will send me to help my fellow-man. Thus the helping of my fellowman can be the evidence because it is seen in my conduct."

Chapter 21

FAITH IN CHRIST LEADS TO LOVE FOR GOD

Do you know what it means to be a child of God and how to get started living a godly life?

In trying to understand the life of a believer it is important to remember that the whole matter of becoming a believer begins with the new birth. We know that the word *believer* refers to a certain kind of people. It is common for us to suppose that they are called believers because they are different from other people. And there is a sense in which that is true, but the difference is not a matter of character or personality. Becoming a child of God is not a matter of improving or changing oneself. It is not even a matter of joining a common program, as I might join a political party. The people who were first called Christians were disciples in Antioch in whom a new life had started. It is not difficult to be born again. It is God who does it, and He will do this for anyone, "whosoever will." However, He does not do it for everybody, but only for those who come to Him through Jesus Christ.

John talks about this in his First Epistle.

> Whosoever believeth that Jesus is the Christ is born of God: and every one that loveth him that begat loveth him also that is begotten of him (1 John 5:1).

This is much more than just identifying certain persons with labels. For instance, "the Christ" refers to the Old Testament promise of a God-appointed way of deliverance. The Old Testament promised that God would deliver His people by sending His own Anointed. The words *anointed* and *Christ* are the same: the One anointed to do a certain task.

God sent His own Son as "the Christ," and through Him God would set up His kingdom. This was intimated in the Old Testament:

> Of which salvation the prophets have inquired and searched diligently, who prophesied of the grace that should come unto you: searching what, or what manner of time the Spirit of Christ which was in them did signify, when it testified beforehand the sufferings of Christ, and the glory that should follow (1 Peter 1:10,11).

Here we have the appointed way — the royal way of life — God's chosen way of deliverance — first suffering, then glory. The prophets who talked about it searched in themselves diligently what this meant when they prophesied of the sufferings of Christ and the glory that was to follow. So the royal way to live is just this: first suffering unto death and then being resurrected.

We will see that this means the way out of this world is by death, and the way into God's world is by resurrection. You will remember the word *Jesus* means the One who was born of a virgin and whose father was God, who was God Himself incarnate, and who came into this world that He might suffer unto death. He was put on the cross and then buried; He was raised from the dead in the Resurrection; He was taken into heaven in the Ascension and is now in the presence of God. He will return to this world in a great blaze of glory. All of this is implied in the name *Jesus*. "Whosoever believeth that Jesus [of Nazareth] is the Christ is born of God." Notice how that verb *believeth* is used: it means continuous acceptance. This is *believeth* in the Old English form, meaning that whoever believes is constantly receiving the new life, which is different from the life which is received when born of man.

We read further: "And every one that loveth him that begat loveth him also that is begotten of him." Now "him that begat" would be God, who begat us by the word of truth; and loving God means to please Him, to keep His Word. "Begotten of him" refers to Christ Jesus, who was begotten of God the Father, and may also refer to other believers, to the brethren.

> By this we know that we love the children of God, when
> we love God, and keep his commandments (1 John 5:2).

This is here, I think, as a practical help; it is assurance about our own conduct. By this we know the will of the children of God: that we love God and keep His commandments. Our response toward God is that we want to please Him — this is our determining principle. In this matter of being a child of God, we plan our activities by looking into the face of Jesus Christ; this is the secret of a believer's approach.

Today a great deal is said about how godly people should act in society. Often the phrase "social action" is used. Set before us are certain activities, various programs in which we are challenged to share. We are told that if we are the children of God, we will do these things. But let us be careful. What will decide what you and I should do is in the face of the Lord Jesus Christ. We will look into His face. Do we really want to please God? Do we really want to obey Him? That is what is required. Everything else will take care of itself.

> For this is the love of God, that we keep his command-
> ments: and his commandments are not grievous (1 John
> 5:3).

"Keeping his commandments" is a phrase that indicates the believer is obedient to God and is seeking to do His will. This is what it means to love God, and it is not an impossible task. We need to remember what Jesus of Nazareth said along this line when He called souls to walk and to work with Him:

> Come unto me, all ye that labour and are heavy laden, and
> I will give you rest. Take my yoke upon you, and learn of
> me; for I am meek and lowly in heart: and ye shall find rest
> unto your souls. For my yoke is easy, and my burden is
> light (Matt. 11:28–30).

Christ's commandments are not grievous. It is not hard to do His will. The Lord does so much for the believer that he is inclined to be well-pleasing in the Lord's sight. Christ wants the believer to do for other people. The Lord has come and given Himself for the believer, who now in turn gives thanks to Him. Giving thanks and praise is acceptable; sharing with and giving to other people is acceptable. This is what He would want the believer to do; and if the love of God is in one's heart, if he personally wants to be well-pleasing in the sight of God, the believer will be eager to be obedient. He will want to do His will, and in this he will not be hurt.

"His commandments are not grievous." John has been discussing what it means to be a child of God. The believer lives the life of faith by starting as a believer, by receiving Jesus Christ into his heart as Savior and Lord.

Chapter 22

OVERCOMING THE WORLD

So many things around us tend to keep us away from God. Do you have any idea how a person can overcome this world in turning to God?

Human life begins in this world. Every person started out as a baby, born into this world in human nature which the Bible calls "the flesh." The baby is in a world that appeals to him through all his senses. He is enmeshed in a situation where he develops appetites, so that he wants things he thinks will feel good. He develops imagination; he wants things of which he likes the looks. He develops pride and self-interest. That is the normal way a human being begins to live, surrounded by things that draw him out to be himself. He becomes interested in himself and in the things he wants and can do. Yet this is sinful, because it is not the way of God.

In being preoccupied with the things of self a man is actually alienated from God. The Bible speaks of him as being lost. If you were to consider again the ordinary baby, think about the way he acts. As he sees and touches things, finally grasping them, what does he do? Am I not right in thinking he tries to get hold of everything he possibly can and take it unto himself? He hangs onto everything he has, regardless of other people.

If you have watched babies (and what you see them doing is not their fault; it is the human nature in them), have you ever noticed how completely self-centered they are? They can smile at you sweetly and do various things that will touch your heart; but the moment you do not let them have their own way, you will find out how they feel. They really want their own way.

The world presents things to the baby that are attractive, and offers things that look nice to him. The world will show him ways in which he can make something of himself; and so the world "eggs him on," leading him to be more and more self-centered all the time. The Christian gospel does not show us how to force the world into being righteous, nor does it offer any procedure which is going to make people naturally different. There is, however, something which the gospel has to say, and this is what we are going to notice now.

> For whatsoever is born of God overcometh the world: and this is the victory that overcometh the world, even our faith (1 John 5:4).

This does not refer to faith as a personal exercise of wisdom as if just anyone can have faith about anything, and so overcome the world. Look at the next verse:

> Who is he that overcometh the world, but he that believeth that Jesus is the Son of God? (1 John 5:5).

Here we need to proceed slowly. Who can be delivered from the appeals of the world? Who can get out of the mesh the world has woven around him, binding him into selfishness and self-centeredness? He who believes in Jesus as the Son of God. The person who believes this can overcome the world. Believing this means that a person will take up his cross and die in the flesh, then he will be raised from the dead, and in this way overcome the world. This is the key to the whole matter of being a child of God.

> This is he that came by water and blood, even Jesus Christ; not by water only, but by water and blood. And it is the Spirit that beareth witness, because the Spirit is truth (1 John 5:6).

These are strange words. Where you see the word *water*, you could think about the preaching of John the Baptist, and where you see the word *blood*, you could think about the work of Jesus Christ. So the person who overcomes the world thinks about the washing away of sin by water; and you can describe this by the word *repentance*. When you think of blood, you can think of the shedding of blood, of the Lamb of God, of Calvary. You can think of dying as a sacrifice. And so in these "strange" words you would have the complete picture of the truth in the gospel. Not only does the believer confess his sins and repent, but he calls himself unworthy because of his sins, and so receives Jesus Christ as his Savior.

When thinking in terms of repentance, the mind is turned inward toward self. When thinking in terms of water, the water is used to wash away that which is evil. When the believer thinks about the blood, he remembers the death of the Lord Jesus Christ. The Bible says in other places, "Repent and believe and you shall receive the promises of God." Here "believe and receive" is what the heart should do toward Christ Jesus. Actually, the person who overcomes the world by faith is the person who repents of sin and who believes that Christ Jesus died on Calvary's cross as his own sacrifice. It is the Spirit who bears witness of these things, because the Spirit is truth. The operation of the Holy Spirit in the heart is evidence that this procedure is effective and has actually worked; because the Spirit is given to those who do so believe, as we have just outlined.

John points out:

> For there are three that bear record in heaven, the Father, the Word, and the Holy Ghost: and these three are one (1 John 5:7).

In speaking of God, we commonly speak of the Father, the Son, and the Holy Ghost. John uses "the Word" here to remind us that Jesus Christ is not only the Son of God; He is also the Word of God.

> And there are three that bear witness in earth, the spirit, and the water, and the blood: and these three agree in one (1 John 5:8).

The three persons of the Godhead in verse 7 are all involved in the salvation experience, and the three that bear witness in earth — here in this world — agree in one. The water represents the ministry of John the Baptist; the blood represents the death of Jesus Christ. John is now emphasizing that the Holy Spirit makes these things real to the heart so as to bring the message to the believer.

In the experience of salvation there are these three elements involved: the Spirit, which is God dealing with us face to face; the water, which is repentance; and the blood, which is death to the flesh and taking up the cross. These are the three aspects of one operation. Throughout this passage the idea is indicated that the things of the world are the things that appeal to a man through his appetite. He is surrounded on every side by things that appeal to him personally — what he likes to eat and drink, what he likes to do, what he would like to have, and finally, what a fine person he is. All these things of the world have within them the elements of sin. They lead the soul away from God. John has been speaking of the soul "that overcometh the world": a person who is delivered from the world. John goes on to point out this is why the person who believes in the Lord Jesus Christ not only confesses sin and with water washes it away, but he accepts Christ's sacrifice for himself as on the cross He shed His blood for sinners.

Chapter 23

FAITH IS GROUNDED IN GOD'S WRITTEN WORD

Is there any way a person can know that God is actually working in his soul?

In dealing with matters of the Christian faith, John emphasizes that Christian living is grounded in faith. It is a matter not only of a personal attitude, but of an inward personal commitment in confidence on a certain promise of God, taking His word about Jesus Christ and what He will do for believers through Him. This matter of having trust in God is an exercise of the soul. It is something the believer does.

Human beings exercise faith as they trust persons who have offered to do something for them. For example, I have faith in a doctor. I do not have faith in every man who is a doctor, but I build up my confidence in one certain doctor and put my trust in him. This means I would go to him, let him examine and prescribe for me, and I would take his medicine. In much the same way, I can put my trust in a mechanic. My car may not be operating right, and I do not want just anyone to handle it; but if I have developed confidence in one man, I feel I can take my car to him with assurance.

Putting trust in God is similar. Throughout this First Epistle, John has emphasized that receiving Jesus Christ as Savior and Lord will bring results in our lives. These results are God's evidence to us. Because of such results we should have confidence in the Lord Jesus Christ.

> If we receive the witness of men, the witness of God is greater (1 John 5:9a).

93

That is, if we can have confidence in a man because we accept evidence about him, the witness about God is greater; it is more obvious. So the person who believes in the Lord Jesus Christ, and thus believes in God through Him, will actually be affected. This is the witness that God gives. It is the real thing. It is not make-believe; it is actually true.

> . . . for this is the witness of God which he hath testified of his Son (1 John 5:9b).

We can now recall all that John has been saying in this Epistle. He is pointing his whole letter toward this idea. He is saying, "This is what I have been talking about: the fact that God gives you evidence of Himself; because if you put your trust in Him, certain results follow. If you believe in the Lord Jesus Christ, if you receive the Son of God into your heart, you will look upon Him as God, and you will want to be pleasing in His sight. That will follow. When God the Father receives you as trusting in His Son, you will receive the Holy Spirit; and the Holy Spirit in your heart will incline you to put your trust in God and to want to please Him. That will follow. This is the witness, the evidence, that you really do belong to God."

> He that believeth on the Son of God hath the witness in himself (1 John 5:10a).

If I believe in the Lord Jesus Christ, so that I believe the Son of God died for the forgiveness of my sins, I feel it inwardly. If a person puts his hand in water, he will know it is wet, and he will know whether the water is hot or cold. Someone else could have told him, and he could have had confidence in that person and taken his word for it, but he would never know as surely as he would if he put his own hand in the water. John argues that we are to have confidence in Jesus Christ not because of what someone tells us, and not because of some argument; we are to have confidence in Him because of our personal relationship with Him. We have walked with Him and trusted in Him, and He has brought certain things to pass.

> He that believeth on the Son of God hath the witness in himself: he that believeth not God hath made him a liar;

because he believeth not the record that God gave of his
Son (1 John 5:10).

When the evidence appears, the conclusion is obvious. Here is
a person who has received Jesus Christ as Savior and Lord, and
because he has received Christ, he begins to worship God. He
now comes to church, he prays to God, he wants to be obedient, and he wants to help his fellowman. If anyone else were
to see that result, he might say that the man was just a good
person. He might say this was the psychological consequence
of certain things the man did. He might even say that this is the
sociological principle prevailing in the community where the
man lives, and that is why these things happen. In so doing he
is actually making God a liar. Anyone who will not accept the
evidence of the results produced in believers as coming from
God is actually denying God who produced the results.

There are people who receive benefits from God and then
either take the glory for themselves or give it to somebody else.
For instance, if I look to God in Christ Jesus and can feel in my
heart that He is forgiving me, I should know that it is done
because Christ died for me. If I have the sense of forgiveness
following the personal receiving of Jesus Christ as my Savior, I
should thank God for it. This is why John writes, "He that
believeth not God hath made him a liar; because he believeth
not the record that God gave of his Son." The record that God
gave of His Son is the consequence in the life of the believer. It
is not just something printed in a book somewhere. The record
is actually what is going on in the believer. This is what John
means when he writes:

And this is the record, that God hath given to us eternal
life, and this life is in his Son (1 John 5:11).

The believer actually has the life of God working in him, and he
ought to thank God for it and give God the glory.

He that hath the Son hath life; and he that hath not the
Son of God hath not life (1 John 5:12).

That is a simple observation, showing two sides of the same
coin. "He that hath the Son hath life." The person who has

received Jesus Christ as Savior has the experience of the life of God working in him. This witness is clear. The soul that receives Jesus Christ suffers unto the death of self and is raised in the newness of life. The person who does receive Jesus Christ has eternal life in his experience. He is obedient to God, and he has love for the brethren in his heart.

> These things have I written unto you that believe on the name of the Son of God; that ye may know that ye have eternal life, and that ye may believe on the name of the Son of God (1 John 5:13).

John has written this whole discussion in his Epistle for the sake of believers, that they might base the assurance of their hearts before God on the fact that God is working in them, and that they might enter even more into the grace that is available. It is possible to have assurance, based on what has happened to the believer. If God is working in his heart, and his own conscience bears witness that he wants to obey Him, to serve Him, and to do for other people, the believer should thank God for this blessing.

Chapter 24

CONFIDENCE IN PRAYING FOR OTHERS

Can you see how personal confidence that one belongs to God strengthens the faith of a believer when he prays to God on behalf of others?

> And this is the confidence that we have in him, that, if we ask any thing according to his will, he heareth us: and if we know that he hear us, whatsoever we ask, we know that we have the petitions that we desired of him (1 John 5:14,15).

John now discusses one of the further consequences of accepting Jesus Christ as Savior and Lord. When the believer accepts Christ Jesus as Savior, he is acceptable to God the Father, who now regenerates him, giving him a new heart. God also gives His Holy Spirit to indwell the regenerated heart of the believer, so that the believer is led from within to willingly walk in the ways of God. Certain consequences will follow that will be proof to the believer himself and to others that he truly belongs to God. Such proof will give him confidence when he prays.

Because the Holy Spirit is leading the yielded believer, the believer's prayers will be in the will of God. Thus the believer can have confidence that his prayers will be heard and his petitions granted.

> If any man see his brother sin a sin which is not unto death, he shall ask, and he shall give him life for them that sin not unto death (1 John 5:16a).

This is one of the most challenging promises in the Bible. How many believers should humbly confess their unbelief to God and ask for more grace! The truth is that Jesus Christ is the propitiation "for the sins of the whole world." He has died for the sins of our loved ones, and carried them away in His own body on the cross.

The believer has every right to pray for the forgiveness of the sins of any loved one. We shall see there is one sin, the unpardonable sin, which is "a sin unto death" for which the believer is not to pray; but the vast majority of sins of which the loved one may be guilty are not unpardonable. Forgiveness is available, and the believer should ask for it. And he can claim the promise that forgiveness and life are available to those for whom he prays in the name of Jesus Christ.

> There is a sin unto death: I do not say that he shall pray for it. All unrighteousness is sin: and there is a sin not unto death (1 John 5:16b,17).

In these words John poses one of the great problems of interpretation in the Bible. He plainly states that "there is a sin unto death" and "there is a sin not unto death." From what he writes it would appear "the sin unto death" is unpardonable, and prayer should not be made for it. However, the sin not unto death is pardonable, and when any believer sees a brother committing such a sin, he should petition the Father for forgiveness. The Bible would instruct the believer to "confess the sin" and to plead the atoning sacrifice of Jesus Christ on the cross on behalf of the sinner.

Further examination of the Scriptures for guidance in the matter of the unpardonable sin will not be undertaken here. John did not elaborate on this point in his Epistle, and it may be wise not to attempt any further exposition in this discussion. That there is such sin is obvious, and that is sobering.

But the reader may take heart that the most of sins of which our loved ones are guilty are probably not unpardonable. They are sins and as such they will condemn the soul unless they are forgiven, so here John challenges all believers to exercise their faith on behalf of their sinning loved ones. Sins can be forgiven because of the death of Jesus Christ on Calvary's cross.

Chapter 25

TURNING FROM EVIL

Do you think a person can ever be sure about being a Christian?

In this First Epistle John has been pointing out that the great truth of the gospel is that God Himself came into human flesh to save the children of men by delivering them from sin through death and then bringing them into eternal life through resurrection. This is the way of life in Christ: dying in the flesh to live in the spirit.

We shall see that in these closing verses of his First Epistle, John strikes certain chords of assurance. There are certain truths the believer can know for sure, and John wants these to be remembered. He wrote the entire Epistle so that believers can be sure they belong to God. He now sums all this up and says in conclusion:

> We know that whosoever is born of God sinneth not; but he that is begotten of God keepeth himself, and that wicked one toucheth him not (1 John 5:18).

This is the confident statement made by John about people who are born of God. Whoever has the life of God working within him, because he has received Jesus Christ as his Savior, does not sin. This does not mean that he never does anything wrong; it means he does not continually practice sin. It is not his desire to do the things that are wrong in the sight of God. If he falls into sins from old habits, that is one thing; if he stumbles into them because of weakness, that is another thing; if he wanders into them because he does not know any better, that is still something else; but his heart and mind bear witness that he does not characteristically want to go contrary to God.

This will be the condition of any person who has received Jesus Christ as Savior and Lord. John has argued in this Epistle the reason that will be the condition of the believer is because "greater is he that is in you than he that is in the world." John is confident that the Lord Jesus Christ, who is alive today and is actively related to those who believe in Him by His Holy Spirit, will gain victory in the believing soul. If any soul has personally received Jesus Christ as his Savior, God has acted to create a new life in that person, and that new life wants to please God. If a person does not have that new life, he does not have the evidence that he belongs to the Lord.

> But he that is begotten of God keepeth himself (1 John 5:18b).

The meaning of this phrase seems to be that he who is begotten of God controls, guards, restrains, and denies himself. The apostle Paul said, "I keep under my body, and bring it into subjection" (1 Cor. 9:27). When John says "the wicked one toucheth him not," he means that Satan cannot get a foothold to tempt the believer. Why not? Because Satan tempts a person with the things that he, in his human nature, likes; but if the believer keeps himself, guards, restrains, and denies himself, and if he puts himself under subjection and reckons himself dead, then Satan cannot get an approach to him.

> And we know that we are of God, and the whole world lieth in wickedness (1 John 5:19).

The believer's consciousness of the indwelling Spirit is such that he knows he is of God and his actions are motivated with the desire to be well-pleasing in God's sight. At the same time he knows that the whole world in which he lives "lieth in wickedness." Common practices that are endorsed and popularized by the public are self-centered, and John is warning believers of this fact and reminding them once more that the whole world, as far as human nature is concerned — in which the lust of the flesh, the lust of the eyes, and the pride of life are in operation — lies in wickedness. People do the things they like, things their pride prompts them to do in their self-centeredness. But believers are not like that; they are motivated by the Holy Spirit to remember the things of Jesus; and by the grace of the Lord Jesus Christ, they are inwardly moved to obey God at whatever expense this may be to themselves.

> And we know that the Son of God is come, and hath given us an understanding, that we may know him that is true, and we are in him that is true, even in his Son Jesus Christ. This is the true God, and eternal life (1 John 5:20).

In this way John summarizes the whole matter. Believers know that the Son of God is come and has given them an understanding, and that they may know Him who is true. They are conscious of the living Lord, and in that awareness they are able to discriminate what man teaches. Can you see what John says there? He has given believers an understanding that they may know "him that is true," and that refers not only to the Lord Jesus Christ, but it also means believers can discriminate among people. They can recognize those who are telling the truth and those who are not. This inner understanding is given to each believer because the Son of God has come.

Jesus Christ is the real truth of God. "This is the true God, and eternal life" is a way of saying this is the truth about God; and this is actually how eternal life operates in us. Note the emphasis when John says, "We are in him that is true, even in his Son Jesus Christ." "In his Son" means that believers accept the life of God into their hearts the way He gave His life into the body of Jesus of Nazareth. Jesus demonstrated that suffering in the flesh was the way to live in the Spirit. "Suffering unto death that he might be raised from the dead." This is the meaning of "Christ": the eternal plan of God promised in the Old Testament. Believers accept this whole truth about Jesus Christ — that a person suffers unto death in order that he might be raised from the dead and live forever. "This is the true God, and eternal life." This is the truth about God. This is actually how eternal life operates in us.

Little children, keep yourselves from idols (1 John 5:21).

It may seem surprising that this admonition is put at the end of the Epistle. And one may wonder why it is off by itself. It has an important meaning: it is a warning. "Idols" are what men make as their own substitution for God. John is saying, "Keep yourselves from human ideas. Keep yourselves from ideas that men conceive." Not all men know Jesus Christ as Savior and Lord. Yet they try to figure things out and offer ideas of their own about God. The believer should keep himself from that. Such ideas may have fragments of truth, but they do not bow down to the Head of the church, to the Lord Jesus Christ; and so they are to be avoided.

Chapter 26

THE BELIEVER WALKS IN TRUTH

Do you have any idea how important it is to know the truth of the Christian gospel?

There are five books in the New Testament that are associated with the name "John." I suspect almost everyone knows about the Gospel of John. Many may think that is the only book written by John, but he also wrote three short Epistles. Both 2 and 3 John were written to individuals: 2 John was apparently written to a woman in the congregation where John served, and 3 John to a man in the congregation where John had been. The fifth book is the Book of Revelation which was given to John. There may be discussion on whether it is the same John each time, but we need not spend time on that question. The material in these books is similar, and there is evidence that the same line of thought is in each one.

> The elder unto the elect lady and her children, whom I love in the truth; and not I only, but also all they that have known the truth; for the truth's sake, which dwelleth in us, and shall be with us for ever (2 John 1,2).

Several things in this passage could be noted. First, no names are mentioned. This may be rather minor, since it could be personal taste. More important is the use of the word *truth*. This word is used several times, and in the following verses it will be used more and more.

> Grace be with you, mercy, and peace, from God the Father, and from the Lord Jesus Christ, the Son of the Father, in truth and love. I rejoiced greatly that I found of

thy children walking in truth, as we have received a
commandment from the Father (2 John 3,4).

In this short portion the word *truth* occurs twice.

There are other matters to be noted in this portion of Scripture. First of all there is "the elder." This is the way the writer
refers to himself. When we think of the word *elder* as it is used
in the New Testament, we have in mind a person who has some
responsibility of teaching and guiding others. The New Testament uses two words interchangeably: *episcopus*, from which
we get the word *bishop* (reflected in the term *episcopal*), and
the word *presbyter,* which we translate by the word *elder.*
Elder really means the "older man." The word *episcopus*
means the "overseer." One might be called a "bishop" at one
time and at another time an "elder," and yet be the same
individual.

This shows us something of the way the early church was
organized within itself. They looked to certain persons among
them for leadership, and such persons were usually men with
experience. They were elder in the sense that they were more
mature, and they exercised an oversight over the other members of the congregation. They were spoken of as being "under
shepherds" and they did the work of the Lord Jesus Christ in a
pastoral sense, caring for the spiritual welfare of the members
of the church who were younger and less experienced. The
elder would be a teaching leader in the church.

"To the elect lady and her children." The word *elect* means
"chosen" and probably referred to the fact that this woman was
of some consequence and had acceptance in the church as a
whole. I am not sure that it refers to her having any particular
position, but it probably does refer to her being one of the
outstanding believers in the group. At any rate, the letter is
written to this woman and her children, probably her house-
hold, no doubt a godly family. One wonders whether she was a
widow. She may have been an outstanding believing woman
who was the leader spiritually in her home, as is often the case.
Evidently it was a family John knew well, and he wanted to let
them know that he really was interested in them.

We shall see that in this short Epistle the writer warns against following unsound teaching, urging these believers not to follow false teachers. This helps us to understand his positive accent upon truth. John says that he loves them in the truth: "whom I love in the truth." This would be loving them as fellow believers, as persons who were walking in the truth. This word *love* does not mean that he liked them particularly or was overjoyed by their company because they were just the kind of people that he was. This will mean *love* in the spiritual and New Testament sense of the word. This word is used to indicate concern for the welfare of the person. When John says "whom I love in the truth," he is speaking of a person in whose welfare he is definitely interested. "And not I only, but also all they that have known the truth"; in other words, he is reminding this woman that she has the loving concern from all the congregation, that is, from all the others who have known the truth.

The word *truth* as it is used in these four verses is used so broadly it could well mean the gospel itself. It could mean the truth about Jesus Christ and all that He means to us, so John could have written, "whom I love in the truth that is in Jesus Christ," in the whole truth about the spiritual realities found in Him. What is this truth in Christ? It would mean that God will come into the human being in grace and mercy to make him a new creature in His Son, and then God would work in him to will and to do His good pleasure. God's grace and mercy will actually work in the individual believer to help him live his life to the praise and glory of God; so the believer will be blessed. This is one way to describe the truth as it is in the gospel of the Lord Jesus Christ.

"For the truth's sake, which dwelleth in us, and shall be with us for ever" (2 John 2) is leading up to something he is going to say later.

Then comes the usual salutation we find in many apostolic letters: "Grace be with you, mercy, and peace." *Grace,* you will remember, is God's doing something for the believer that he does not deserve; God's giving him favor he has not earned.

Mercy is God's kindness to a person when he could be at fault. God's faithfulness and grace are given to the believer at a time when he may have acted so as to have forfeited the favor of God; but God shows him mercy and peace — the peace that passes all understanding, which He gives to those who put their trust in Him.

> Grace be with you, mercy, and peace, from God the Father, and from the Lord Jesus Christ, the Son of the Father, in truth and love (2 John 3).

When John talks about God, he refers to God the Father. Grace, mercy, and peace come to the believer from God the Father, not God the Creator, not God the Almighty, and not God the Lord of all nations. As long as the believer is in that relationship with God where he is a child of God and God is his Father — a relationship which is in Christ Jesus — then grace, mercy, and peace will be with him "from the Lord Jesus Christ, the Son of the Father." Notice that when John refers to the Lord Jesus Christ, he gives Him His whole title: He is the Lord of all; He is Jesus, the One who died for us and who saves us; He is Christ, the One whom God sent to do His work. But then John uses the phrase "the Son of the Father." John brings out the fact of the sonship of Christ; the fact that Jesus Christ is the Son of God and this grace is to be to the believer from Him. "In truth and love" refers to truth according to God's plan — the way in which God actually wants to give it to believers.

> I rejoiced greatly that I found of thy children walking in truth, as we have received a commandment from the Father (2 John 4).

Thus John expresses this word of appreciation and commendation to this woman, because he has found her children walking in truth. It is implied they have been living their lives in the relationship with God which comes from recognizing Jesus Christ as Savior, and that in Him believers do belong to God, and God does belong to them. John found this family walking and living that way.

Chapter 27

LOVE FOR THE BRETHREN

Do you realize that if you were really doing the will of God, you would be helping other people in the Christian gospel?

As we have been studying this letter, we have seen that John was paying special attention to "truth," and emphasizing to the recipient that he appreciated the fact that her children were walking in truth. John wanted her to know that his interest in her and in her family was all in the truth. John evidently was putting emphasis on the word *truth* because the entire letter has the nature of a warning. He warned that they should not follow men who were not telling the truth about the Lord Jesus Christ. In this as in other matters of faith we can get all kinds of ideas about anything, and I often think that it is particularly difficult for a person to come to believe the gospel because he hears so many different ideas about it. If a person tries to understand about the Lord Jesus Christ, he will hear so many different ideas from various people that he could never sift them out to decide which is right. Only by the grace of God can a person ever come to faith.

In this letter John has indicated that he had a special interest in this particular woman and her family. He warns them about associating with people who are not keeping themselves in line with the truth of God. In the opening verses, he has emphasized the fact that he is interested in their staying in the truth. He testifies that he has great joy: "I rejoiced greatly that I found of thy children walking in truth, as we have received a commandment from the Father."

But in the next few verses John concentrates on something

else. The New Testament often urges believers to speak the truth in love. Sometimes this expression is used: "the truth and love."

> Grace be with you, mercy, and peace, from God the Father, and from the Lord Jesus Christ, the Son of the Father, in truth and love (2 John 3).

Having emphasized "truth" in the first four verses, John now focuses on the reality of "love" in the whole matter. It is to be understood that the truth of God leads believers into love for God and for man.

> And now I beseech thee, lady, not as though I wrote a new commandment unto thee, but that which we had from the beginning, that we love one another (2 John 5).

In effect John is saying, "I will have you understand in my writing to you that this is one thing we want to keep clear: what we really want to do is to seek the welfare of others. When we love one another, we try to work things out that are best for each other."

> And this is love, that we walk after his commandments. This is the commandment, That, as ye have heard from the beginning, ye should walk in it. For many deceivers are entered into the world, who confess not that Jesus Christ is come in the flesh. This is a deceiver and an antichrist (2 John 6,7).

Discussions about the truth so often become a lot of talk. This is a danger, almost a handicap, in trying to deal with people about the things of the Lord. There are times when a person talks to others about spiritual things when they will say, "Oh, he has come to talk religion." As soon as someone uses that phrase, others become uneasy and will often start an argument. It is easy to flounder into argument when talking about the truth of the gospel; and argument can become very involved because words have so many meanings. Often a person will say something that makes sense to him, but to the other person it does not make sense at all. This could be the beginning of an argument. Arguments like this often become personal, and when that is the case, they become heated.

Unfortunately there is often far more heat than light in the course of such arguments. Emotions are aroused and the misunderstandings are not cleared up.

This is a feature of much that is in the field of testimony about faith. The result is that many people make it a rule never to argue religion, because they have seen that much harm can come, and little benefit. It is no wonder, then, that John makes it a point to emphasize that the original commandment, the basic truth, is that we love one another. We should remember that this phrase "love one another" does not mean that persons need to like one another. It would be wonderful if people *could* like one another. But the fact is we usually only like those who are like us. Because people are so different from each other, they often do not like one another; yet that is no reason they could not love one another.

Love is not a matter of sentiment; love is what a person does for other people. "And this is love, that we walk after his commandments" (2 John 6), that is, that we obey the will of God. Walking in love is a matter of walking in humble, simple obedience to the guidance of the living Lord. How can that be love? Believers will be doing what is pleasing in the sight of God; and this means they will be helpful to other men, because God loves people and wants to help them. If I do what God wants me to do, I will do no one any harm, but rather I will actually help others. This is love: that I walk after His commandments.

In studying the First Epistle of John, we found that walking according to the commandments is not a matter of memorizing a number of rules and regulations and then keeping them. This phrase "walking after his commandments" can be summed up simply as obeying the Lord Jesus Christ, walking in the Holy Spirit, letting Him show the believer His way. These "commandments" He would show us are not expressed like the Ten Commandments, but they are the inward guidance that enables the believer to walk in the way He leads us.

This is what is meant when the Scriptures speak of loving others. If a believer wanted to help someone, how would he do it? He would help him the way the Lord Jesus leads him, in a way that would be most helpful to that person. As humans we do not understand everything, nor do we always know what is best for another person. We might see someone in a certain situation and think he needs money, when what he really needs is friendship or some advice. Maybe what that man needs is criticism or guidance of some sort, but how would we as believers know? Which of these things should we do? That is what the Lord Jesus by the Holy Spirit would lead us to know.

A believer may have children or teen-agers in the home. Does he love them? Loving them would not mean letting them do anything they wanted to do, allowing them to go their own way. Rather, loving them would mean that the believer would try to guide them and help them to understand what they should do.

In love, believers will live according to the commandments of the Lord as they are led. For instance, even if a mother wants to help her sick child, sometimes the doctor will encourage the mother not to come to the hospital. The mother might want to take the child outside, whereas the doctor would tell her to leave the child alone. Perhaps she might wish to give the child something to eat, as it would give her great pleasure to see the child enjoy himself. But if she really loved the child, she would follow the doctor's orders. This would be love: "that we walk after his commandments." The believer would do what God wants him to do.

> For many deceivers are entered into the world, who confess not that Jesus Christ is come in the flesh. This is a deceiver and an antichrist (2 John 7).

When we say that Jesus Christ has come in the flesh, we mean that in Jesus of Nazareth, God's way of doing things, which we sum up under the word *Christ,* was manifested. That is the truth, as He walked in obedience; and this is shown to us. If we believe in Him and His Spirit is in us, He moves us to walk in obedience. The pattern of Jesus Christ is actually the pattern of the truth. This is the truth, and anyone who does not say what John is saying is antichrist.

Chapter 28

FELLOWSHIP WITH TRUE BELIEVERS

Do you think it should make any difference to a believer what another person is teaching about the gospel?

The popular notion that it makes no difference what a person believes just as long as he is sincere can be most misleading. John deals with this in this letter to the woman with her children. He is anxious for them to learn that it does make a difference with whom they have fellowship. It makes a difference what kind of person they endorse with their good will and with their friendship. It could be easy for people to think it would not make any difference as long as that person was talking about the Bible or teaching the gospel — that should certainly be all right.

Often people have the notion that as long as a person is teaching a Sunday school class, everything he says must be all right, and he should be free to say it. There is abroad in our land a general feeling of permissive liberty. We almost think it is wrong to check up on what another person says or teaches. And yet that is foolish, because if in our understanding of the gospel and Christian life we agree that a believer should be a person who accepts Jesus Christ, it certainly does make a difference what he believes. What he believes will depend on what he hears, and that in turn will depend on what he is taught. It all comes back to the teacher, and therefore it is important that believing parents should be careful what they endorse.

This is brought out clearly by John:

> Look to yourselves, that we lose not those things which
> we have wrought, but that we receive a full reward (2 John
> 8).

John felt that the work he had done in teaching the gospel, and
the effort he had put forth in getting this family to come to
where they were in their faith, could now be lost if they chose
some other way of believing. He warned them that it would be
easy to be misled, and that real loss would occur if they were
led away from the faith that is in Christ Jesus.

> Whosoever transgresseth, and abideth not in the doctrine
> of Christ, hath not God (2 John 9a).

Ordinarily the word *transgression* refers to someone's step-
ping out of bounds or backing away from what he should do; but
in this particular case the language seems to apply to the person
who moves ahead of what he should do, one who goes beyond
what is taught in the gospel. When a person is not staying
within the teaching in the Bible concerning Christ Jesus, he is
transgressing. Such a person "hath not God."

You would be surprised how many times people begin their
Christian lives by reading, studying, and believing the Bible,
when someone comes along and proposes that he knows more
than what is in the Bible. He says the Bible is all right for a
start, but he has developed in the meantime and now has a
better understanding; he has learned new things so that he has
arrived at conclusions which the Bible does not present. This is
a matter of transgression.

The doctrine of Christ means the doctrine that was lived out
in Jesus of Nazareth, the teaching that is in Him. This is a
teaching which indicates that the soul should be yielded to God
personally: the will should be committed to Him. The actions
of the believer should be in obedience to the will of God, as it is
mediated by the Holy Spirit through Jesus Christ right now. In
other words, the doctrine of Christ would be the kind of
teaching that would be based on a personal, living relationship
with the almighty God through Christ Jesus by the Holy Spirit.

It is difficult to detect what teachers may have in their minds
or hearts. We can only go by what they say. Do they say things

that imply that they are personally in fellowship with the Lord Jesus Christ? Do they say they have personally taken the time to look into His face? Are they encouraging you to look personally into the face of the Lord Jesus Christ, and to walk hand in hand with Him? Or does the teacher think the Lord Jesus Christ lived two thousand years ago and left His pattern so that now we just go from there, developing it as we see fit? This second line of teaching is different from the first, and this is what John has in mind when he warns that believers should be careful not to follow such instruction.

The person who abides in the doctrine of Christ is in personal relationship with His Father at all times. At any time, whether on the seashore or on the hilltop, the believer can lift up his face unto heaven and say, "Our Father," and the soul that lives this way "hath both the Father and the Son." That person is in fellowship with God as Father, and with Jesus Christ as the Son of God. The Lord Jesus is actually functioning in him as the Son of God and inclining that person to look toward God as Father.

> If there come any unto you, and bring not this doctrine, [any person who is teaching anything that is not according to the actual life and performance of Jesus of Nazareth], receive him not into your house, neither bid him God speed [this is a strong admonition that is given to each of us. We are to have nothing to do with anybody who offers another gospel]: for he that biddeth him God speed is partaker of his evil deeds (2 John 10,11).

This is something we need to take to our hearts and minds seriously. When I encourage someone to teach and he does not teach the truth, I am partially responsible for what that man does; I am a partaker with him of his evil deeds, of his wrongdoing. We may have someone in the Sunday school who is not teaching the gospel of Jesus Christ. He may teach that we should live like Christ and that Christianity as a whole is a cultural pattern that society should adopt. He may teach about the nations of the world, or what should be told the government of our country. These things Jesus Christ did not do, and if you give your personal influence and support to that person, you are a partaker with him of his evil deeds.

I hope you will understand that I am aware of how serious this admonition is and how close it comes to us, because every day we deal with people of various views. People do not like to be evaluated; they do not like to have their views appraised. They resent being asked what they believe because they think they should be accepted anyway; but this Second Epistle of John makes it clear that you and I cannot accept that. We can only accept them when they teach the truth as it is in Jesus of Nazareth: the living God in the human being; the living God in personal fellowship with His child here upon earth; the child of God in personal fellowship with God the Father, and the child of God yielded to God the Father and doing His will. This is what should be taught.

There is a personal word in the last part of this Epistle:

> Having many things to write unto you, I would not write with paper and ink: but I trust to come unto you, and speak face to face, that our joy may be full (2 John 12).

Here we have another wonderful thought about Christian life and experience: we need personal fellowship. We need to have contact with other Christian people on an individual basis, and especially with the people who see the things of the Lord in the same way we do. It is a blessing. So John ends his letter by saying: "The children of thy elect sister greet thee. Amen" (2 John 13). And in this Epistle we have had a serious word spoken to us as believers by this faithful servant.

Chapter 29

HELPING THE BRETHREN

Do you realize how important it is to encourage those who are teaching the truth about Christ?

We will now turn in our study to the Third Epistle of John. The Second and Third Epistles of John are alike in that each was written to one person instead of to a church. The Second Epistle was apparently written to a woman and her family; the Third Epistle is written to a man. It begins by saying: "The elder unto the well-beloved Gaius, whom I love in the truth" (v. 1). Here again the focus is on conduct. Both 2 John and 3 John guide believers in their dealings with other believers. In his Second Epistle John was anxious to warn against an easy acceptance of anyone. He wanted believers to be careful whom they endorsed. He warned against accepting unsound doctrine, stating that it makes a difference as to what a person teaches, what he stands for in other teaching of the gospel.

In his Second Epistle John was actually saying to the elect lady that she should not receive into her house nor grant the good will of her personal fellowship to persons who were teaching anything other than the simple truth that is in Jesus Christ. Here in 3 John the attention is on another aspect of this relationship. Believers are encouraged to be helpful to others, especially to strangers.

> The elder unto the well-beloved Gaius, whom I love in the truth. Beloved, I wish above all things that thou mayest prosper and be in health, even as thy soul prospereth. For I rejoiced greatly, when the brethren came and testified of the truth that is in thee, even as thou walkest in the truth (3 John 1–3).

This is a letter of commendation and encouragement. John begins by saying to this man that he loves him dearly. He uses the phrase "in the truth" several times. He is not using this phrase to imply that what he is saying should be heeded because he is sincere and honest. What he is saying is in *the* truth, that is understood to be the truth of the gospel. The truth of the gospel would refer to the believer's actual experience in Christ. Gaius was evidently a true believer, and John could say "whom I love in the truth," meaning he loved him as a fellow believer, because he was a genuine child of God. John knew that this was a man in whom the Holy Spirit was making the things of Jesus Christ active and strong.

> Beloved, I wish above all things that thou mayest prosper and be in health, even as thy soul prospereth (3 John 2).

Apparently this man's soul was prospering, and John was simply saying he wished this man would be as fortunate in everything else as he was in spiritual matters. John's thought seems to be a little clearer in the third verse: "For I rejoiced greatly, when the brethren came and testified of the truth that is in thee, even as thou walkest in the truth." This tells us that the prosperity of the soul — the wholesome, sound, healthy condition of a Christian soul — will follow obedience to the will of God. In the next verse John implies that Gaius' soul was prospering because he walked in the truth, obeying the will of God, and John wished that he might be blessed in everything.

When the brethren testified of the truth in Gaius, they were not talking about the truth that this man talked about or what he had expressed in some argument. They were talking about the way he lived. They testified to the truth that he manifested in his living "even as thou walkest in the truth." John brings this out again in the fourth verse when he says, "I have no greater joy than to hear that my children walk in truth," which is to say, when they live in the truth of the gospel, in a personal relationship to God made available through the gospel of Jesus Christ.

> Beloved, thou doest faithfully whatsoever thou doest to the brethren, and to strangers; which have borne witness

of thy charity before the church: whom if thou bring
forward on their journey after a godly sort, thou shalt do
well: because that for his name's sake they went forth,
taking nothing of the Gentiles (3 John 5–7).

These verses indicate the particular situation in which Gaius
had been exercising himself. Apparently there were certain
persons who were traveling through the church, perhaps as
traveling evangelists or missionaries. They were brethren in
the Lord even though they were strangers in that congregation, and Gaius had evidently helped them, possibly on the
basis of their personal testimony to Jesus Christ.

The word *faithfully* does not necessarily mean quite what
we have in mind when we use that word. We usually use that
term when a man keeps a trust and we can depend on him. We
have in mind a man who will continue always to do what he says
he will do. But here we should look at the word *faithfully* as we
look at the word *faith*. The life style followed by Gaius was full
of faith — faith that was exercised for the brethren and for
strangers. These people throughout the church afterwards
talked about what Gaius had done for them. They bore witness
to his charity. We should note again that the word *charity*, as
John used it, does not refer to an inward attitude, nor is it a
kindness or a mildness that a man might have in his own soul. It
refers to what he is actually doing for others. It is food, shelter,
and clothing, something he had shared. These traveling serv-
ants of the Lord went among other believers and told everyone
what Gaius had done for them. John tells Gaius that he had
served the Lord when he helped these brethren who had gone
out in the service of the Lord.

We therefore ought to receive such, that we might be
fellow-helpers to the truth (3 John 8).

This verse refers to believers who were maintaining themselves as witnesses. They were going about witnessing to the
gospel, not counting on unbelievers for support. Money was
probably involved, but certainly support meant more than
money. These were brethren who may well have gone out
without popular support and approval; they may have been

subject to criticism. Gaius would be one of the people who supported them. They may have gone out without the fellowship of all believers.

There are persons who are called to live as children of God, witnessing to the Lord, even though some will not associate with them or support them. But Gaius was the kind of believer who did have fellowship and gave support. Believers are told that they ought to receive such that they might be fellow helpers to the truth, as Gaius was. It is important for believers to give their personal help to others who are maintaining a testimony for the truth of the gospel in Jesus Christ. In this part of his Third Epistle, John has spoken words of praise to a man who helped other believers, even strangers, when they came into the community. It was done openly and the good word had gone abroad. Word had been spread around that this kind of fraternal help was good, not only because of the reputation of Gaius, but because the witnesses so helped were good people; and this was a matter of supporting and encouraging people who actually were serving the Lord. If we give to people who are serving the Lord, we actually share in their service.

Chapter 30

WALKING IN HUMILITY AND VIRTUE

In the latter part of this Third Epistle, John is commenting further on Gaius' treatment of traveling witnesses to the Lord. He takes this occasion to comment on the attitude of certain individuals in the church. In the testimony of the gospel, the individual does make a difference. A believer's conduct does matter in the sight of God. In this short passage two individuals are referred to: one whom John criticizes and another whom John approves and praises.

> I wrote unto the church: but Diotrephes, who loveth to have the preeminence among them, receiveth us not (3 John 9).

In the next verse is a description of this man who was evidently prominent in the congregation, but who had personal resentment against John. Why? We do not know. It is intimated that he was jealous of John. Here was a man who in his place of leadership enjoyed superiority. Unfortunately there are such persons; they are given some responsibility in the congregation, and then become proud in that position, favoring certain persons and hindering others.

In this case John had written to the church to encourage them to receive some itinerant witnesses. Diotrephes, who loved "to have the preeminence" in the congregation, was probably jealous of John, and so he had opposed helping these strangers. This is often seen when working with a group of people. It is most unfortunate. One person may not like another person, and it will often follow that he opposes everything the other supports. Something like that is implied here. Because Diotrephes loved to have preeminence among them, he did not want to receive the travelers. He was not willing to give John any status of leadership in the congregation. He was not willing to concede that John had anything to say that would be significant to the congregation. John does not excuse him for this attitude and says that he will deal more specifically with this man when he comes to them.

> Wherefore, if I come, I will remember his deeds which he doeth, prating against us with malicious words: and not content therewith, neither doth he himself receive the brethren, and forbiddeth them that would, and casteth them out of the church (3 John 10).

This, then, is what Diotrephes did. Not only did he discredit John, but he opposed the program John had set up. He would not personally receive the brethren; and he also forbade anyone else to receive them, even thrusting them out of the church. Here was a man who did not like John, and because of that he not only would not do what John asked, but he was against missions since John was in favor of them. This is a common tragedy in congregational life. It has been my privilege to be a minister of the gospel for a number of years, and there have been congregations and other places where, if my name were mentioned as a possible speaker, there would be individuals who did not want me to be invited to come. They did not know anything about me except what I stand for: I believe that the Bible is the Word of God and what it says to be the truth, and I teach that. They did not want to hear that. That is the sort of thing Diotrephes had been doing.

A man like that is no help to the church, even as he is no help to anyone. He is a hindrance because of his influence on others. In verse 11 John makes a general statement for us to keep in mind when thinking about someone like that: "Beloved, follow not that which is evil, but that which is good." If a man's general attitude is so negative and contrary that he is opposed to things for no good reason, we can be sure that he is probably opposed solely because of personal feelings. In that case we can keep in mind what John is saying here: How will we know when a man is good? "By their fruits ye shall know them." This does not always mean we can tell by the number of converts he has or the size of the church he serves, but it does mean we can tell by the way he talks whether or not he is talking in a way that is agreeable or not to the Lord Jesus Christ.

> Beloved, follow not that which is evil, but that which is good. He that doeth good is of God: but he that doeth evil hath not seen God (3 John 11).

Here John is bringing to our minds a great truth: our experience and our testimony in the Lord is individual.

It is a wonderful thing to belong to a large, missionary-minded church. It may be true that in your congregation a great deal of money is raised because the people are generous, and a large portion of it given to missions. The members of the congregation conduct themselves in such a way that they leave the impression of faithful witness to the Lord Jesus Christ. In this Third Epistle John says that if you join that church it will be a real comfort to you and a great help; but that will not be enough. You must stand for these things personally. You need to deal with the Lord Jesus Christ on an individual basis. Demetrius is an example of what John means about this when he says, "Demetrius hath good report of all men." If a person lives honestly, sincerely, and faithfully, everyone will notice it and speak well of him.

> I had many things to write, but I will not with ink and pen write unto thee: but I trust I shall shortly see thee, and we shall speak face to face. Peace be to thee. Our friends salute thee. Greet the friends by name (3 John 13,14).

Notice the individual, personal touch. It is wonderful to belong to a big, strong church, but are you personally strong in your faith? It is great to belong to a Bible class that is really studying the Bible, but are you studying the Bible for yourself? Perhaps you belong to a church that emphasizes yielding to the Lord and seeking His face, but do *you* seek the face of the Lord Jesus Christ? Perhaps the church you belong to promotes prayer meetings; but do *you* pray? This is the personal note we find in this Third Epistle. John indicates this even as he closes the letter: "Greet the friends by name." One by one.

Just as believers have been warned in the Second Epistle not to lightly or easily accept anyone in the Lord, so in this Third Epistle believers have been encouraged to really help the brethren and to do things for them. Believers should stand by those who are proclaiming and teaching the truth. They should extend their fellowship, comradeship, and encouragement in every way possible. This will be pleasing to the Lord.

DATE DUE

12/11/13			

The Library Store   #47-0103